Books by Sylvester Nemes
  The Soft-Hackled Fly
  The Soft-Hackled Fly Addict

THE Soft-Hackled Fly Addict
BY SYLVESTER NEMES

Including a short story by the author:
Upper Big Blue

STACKPOLE BOOKS

Copyright © 1981 by Sylvester Nemes

Published in 1993 by
STACKPOLE BOOKS
5067 Ritter Road
Mechanicsburg, PA 17055

All rights reserved, including the right to reproduce this book or portions thereof in any form or by any means, electronic or mechanical, including photocopying, recording, or by any information storage and retrieval system, without permission in writing from the publisher. All inquiries should be addressed to Stackpole Books, 5067 Ritter Road, Mechanicsburg, Pennsylvania 17055.

Printed in the United States of America

10 9 8 7 6 5 4 3 2 1

Library of Congress Cataloging-in-Publication Data

Nemes, Sylvester.
    The soft-hackled fly addict / by Sylvester Nemes ; including a short story by the author, Upper big blue.
    Originally published: Chicago, IL : S. Nemes, © 1981.
      p.   cm.
  ISBN 0-8117-1671-6 : $19.95
    1. Flies, Artificial. 2. Fly fishing. I. Title.
SH451.N4   1993
799.1'755—dc20   93-12707
                                                                         CIP

This one's for Hazel

Contents

Introduction	9
Chapter 1: Masters of the Soft-Hackled Fly: Pritt and Edmonds and Lee	15
Chapter II: Pritt's patterns	23
Chapter III: Pritt on fishing, and the case of the bloas	61
Chapter IV: Edmonds and Lee: Matching artificials to naturals	71
Chapter V: Modern, soft-hackled fly fishing methods	79
Chapter VI: Soft-hackled flies, revisited and refined	95
Chapter VII: Upper Big Blue — A short story	*111*

Introduction

The name and idea for this book came from correspondence between myself and Paul Brown, who tries to live year round in West Yellowstone, Montana. Paul is one of those irrepressible characters who thinks that fly fishing is a major reason for living. For a time he was teaching school in that junction so that he could live according to his reason.

We met there in the fall of 1977, and he wrote to me several times to let me know how the fishing progressed to the end of the park season, October 31, and then after it on longer-seasoned state waters. He resisted the soft-hackled fly for nearly two years, but in the fall of 1979, after I left, he decided to try it. His letter, dated October 19, tells what happened. ". . . we've been getting fish when no one else has—all on soft hackles. I think my problem has been one of a lack of confidence in them. After deciding to give them a fair trial, they have been producing. I fished with four other anglers the other day and took four fish in an hour when they got nothing (on a number 12 partridge and claret). I think with the fair trial I've been giving them, I'm beginning to learn how to fish them. One has to 'feel' them through the water and get the fish up by an effort of the will. It helps. A patterned casting is helping, too, I think. You must try to get the fly moving just right through a particular section of water."

From his letter, I felt that Paul was hooked on soft hackles. My immediate response to him was approximately: "once you become addicted to the fly, you'll find it difficult to fish anything else." From the word, "addicted," of course, came the last word of the title. The idea for the book was born there, too, although at that time I didn't know what shape it would take.

I wrote recently to Paul to try to retrieve the letter in which I believed the above excerpt to be written. I also asked him if he could remember what he had written in his letter, because, at the time, I could not find it. Paul could not put his hands on my letter, and not knowing that I had found his, offered to reconstruct the 'gist' of the letter into a new one, just received. Part of it is included here because it contains a slightly different and more interesting statement about soft hackles.

"As you recall, I fished predominantly with stonefly nymphs and streamers, the conventional wisdom for the fall fish, and did not give the S. H. a decent trial. Until the season's end I fished with S. H.'s exclusively. My initial impression was that I felt like an idiot, 'just heave the thing out there and wait for it to swing around.' I remember, too, thinking I would not long continue to fish in this fashion because I felt I was being robbed of any contributions I might have made in order to fish the fly more effectively. In short, it seemed an idiot's method, offering plenty of time to think about things other than fishing. The light dawned after some practice, when I felt I could actually 'feel' the progress of the fly down the river and through what I considered good holding lies. It was at this point that suddenly I became 'alive' to the entire drift of the fly, and no longer felt that 'vacant' period of uselessness until the line came fully taught at the end of the swing. I think this was the appeal for me; that tenuous, non-direct 'connection' with the fly's progress, as opposed say, to fishing a streamer on a tight line. The 'indirect connection' provided the sense of mystery that for me is the primary charm of the S. H."

Paul is a noteworthy example of the way anglers are turned around by the fly and its simple philosophy. With Paul, I met three of his very good angling friends, all of whom did not fish the soft hackle before I met them. They were all fly fishing experts, however, stealing into private spring creeks to fish tiny dries (don't worry, owners, they never killed a fish), scaling precipitous rock walls to fish unfished portions of great trout rivers, and chasing hatch after hatch all over the west.

One of their favorite fall patterns around West Yellowstone, as Paul pointed out, was a two-inch long, heavily weighted stone fly nymph. They demolished brand new graphite rods with it. They pelted themselves in the head, shoulders, and body with it. (Lucky for them one of them was nearly through med school). They cursed the fishing style required to fish it. And, of course, they caught fish with it. When I fished alongside them with my floating line and sparse soft hackles, I caught fish, too, sometimes less but oftentimes more. I was having more fun, though. The angler who noticed this first was Paul. "You stay right in there with those little flies, don't you?" he said once to me as I released an upper, teen-sized brown.

The following fall season, Paul was still living according to his reason. Only two of his friends were on the rivers (the med student was interning in Oregon). When we went to our favorite river, they were all fishing soft hackles.

I think I can safely say that nearly every fly fisherman I introduced to the soft hackle, was, the next time I saw him, using the fly most of the time. By now, that number is in the hundreds. And by now, anglers by the thousands are addicted to these simple, sober and ancient patterns.

The soft-hackled fly is now being written about frequently. Professional guides tell me it often saves the day for them and their clients. Avowed dry fly fishermen are using them upstream, and tackle outlets like Bailey, Lilley, Barnes and Kaufmann and many others sell them by the score.

It wasn't until I purchased copies of "North-Country Flies," 1886, by T. E. Pritt and "Brook and River Trouting," 1916, by Edmonds and Lee, in 1980, that the shape of this book took form. I had looked long and hard for these two books. When I found them, I thought I would share the colored plates, dressings, and fishing methods of both books with other soft-hackled fly addicts.

The reason for this is obvious. Pritt is considered by angling historians to be the godfather of this type of fly. Edmonds and Lee, too, are quoted frequently in angling literature pertaining to soft hackles. So all of Pritt's plates and one from Edmonds and Lee form the nucleus of this book. I could be wrong about the emphasis on Pritt, because Edmonds and Lee's book has just been reprinted in England, while Pritt's book has never been, to my knowledge.

There are other reasons for this book. When my first book, "The Soft-Hackled Fly" was published in 1975, I was anxious to get into print. Also, the publisher was not inclined to wait for me to "think out" my first book completely. The section of the book which suffered the most was the one on fishing, or the actual casting of the fly and presentation, particularly in problem water. This area is now covered fully by 14 pages of new material.

You will also find several new soft hackle patterns developed by myself and other friendly addicts. There are new, easier tying instructions, and the introduction of new materials. There is the announcement that previously rare materials for soft hackles can now be easily imported into this country. There is an attempt to match soft hackles to living insect orders, thanks to Edmonds and Lee and some suggestions by Carl Richards. And there is an unpublished short story which some readers may feel is pertinent to the soft-hackled fly.

I have been called evangelistic by some anglers in my attempts to establish the soft hackle as a true, American angling form. I hope this book continues the crusade.

Thanks are due to many people for their help, encouragement, and cooperation. They are not being named in order of importance. My wife, Hazel. My son, Eric. Dean Yannias. Paul Brown. Angelo Sardina. Al Adas. Phil and Dotty Noerenberg. Dave Kilmer. And Carl Richards.

Chapter I:

Masters of the Soft-Hackled Fly: Pritt and Edmonds and Lee

I was immensely pleased when during the summer of 1980, I received copies of "North-Country Flies," by T. E. Pritt; and "Brook and River Trouting," by Harfield H. Edmonds and Norman N. Lee. And I was highly elated when I opened the books for the first time, for here before me were the two books, which, I believe, communally form the bible of the soft-hackled fly.

Both books are beautifully illustrated in color, the first by hand painting and the second by colored photographs. Both books are difficult to find and expensive when they are obtainable. My search for the two copies lasted several years. I had seen one or the other advertised from time to time, but I always thought they were too expensive. Young Tony Lyons found them for me through his used angling book company. He said "North-Country Flies," came from Preston Jenning's library, which added much importance to my owning it.

When I first started thinking about the "Addict," and after I found these two books, I thought it would be a good idea to include, word for word, the entire bodies of the works pertaining to fly fishing. I say this because both books have sections in them relating to other kinds of fishing, such as bustard fishing, minnow spinning, creeper and stone fly fishing, and upstream worm fishing. These are all bait fishing methods except bustard fishing, which is a form of nocturnal fly fishing. The method is described by T. E. Pritt: "The bustard is a large moth, white or brown, and may be dressed thus on a No. 4 or 5 hook. The White Bustard: wings from a White Owl's quill feather, body white Berlin wool, ribbed with yellow silk, or gold tinsel; head, black Ostrich herl, used sparingly; legs, from a white cock's hackle. The Brown Bustard is thus dressed; wings, from a quill or tail feather of a Brown Owl; body, brown fur from a hare's neck, mixed with a little common worsted, and any brown hackle run all the way up it.

". . . . Bustard fishing demands an equal amount of self-denial and general discomfort to which the writer, at least, is not equal, but very heavy baskets of large fish are often made by it when no other bait is looked at. Armed with one, or both of the moths described above, with a spare cast round your hat in case of accident, using a cast about six feet long, and throwing a line not much, if any, longer than your rod, you begin fishing as soon as it is perfectly dark. Trout will rarely take the bustard in the dusk, and on a summer's night, which is your only bustard time, you need scarcely look for sport much before midnight.

". . . . By far the best fishing with this lure, and it is perhaps worthier of the angler's art, is had between dawn and sunrise in the roughish streams and rapids; then, of course, you must wade. Trout often rise ravenously at the moth in the very early morning, but the game is up at the same moment of the sun."

I know at least a half a dozen Michigan locals who still fish in the manner described above. The method produces big browns, particularly during the nocturnal, hexagenia hatch and for some weeks after it.

The inclusion of bait fishing methods in classic, English angling literature was quite common in the late 19th and early 20th centuries. Pritt and Edmonds and Lee did it. Cutcliffe did it. And Stewart and others did it. Obviously, it was no disgrace to mix fishing methods, as it still is no disgrace, today, in England to do so. Now, on salmon rivers where both fly and spinning are permitted, some anglers come to the river with a fly rod and a spinning rod. If one method doesn't work, the angler tries the other.

In America, today, this is all changed. Now you have to declare yourself a dry fly man, a nymph man, a streamer man, a stonefly man, a wet fly man, or heaven forbid, a soft hackle man. You have to choose sides and be careful who you talk to about the side you've chosen. We are all pedants. Just last year I was fishing a carrier of the lower Madison river with a new friend. We fished soft hackles for two days and ended up on this carrier when a hatch occurred bringing the trout to the surface. I changed to dries, turned upstream and took two nice fish. My friend looked at me, a little astonished. "You're a pretty good dry fly fisherman, too," he said.

Pritt's aim in writing his book is best described in his preface to the first edition of 1885. It is titled, "Yorkshire Trout Flies." "It occurred to me, some three or four years ago, that there was again room in this great angling county for a book which should not only give the dressings and seasons of trout flies, but also add the best possible aid in the form of illustrations carefully and accurately coloured, in order to convey to the eye of the beholder correct impressions of the size, shape and colour of those artificial flies which experience has proved are best adapted to the Yorkshire waters. It is a long stretch from the days of Theakston and Jackson to this present time, and in the interval there has grown up amongst observant anglers a decided preference for hackled flies, and wisely so, and this preference is by no means confined within the limits of our county."

In his preface to the second edition, in 1886, Pritt says, "The first edition of this work was published under the title of 'Yorkshire Trout Flies.' It was very generously received, and was quickly exhausted. But it was pointed out in quarters entitled to high respect that the title was too local; that the patterns of flies would do good service on all northern waters; that they would kill grayling as well as trout; and that the remarks upon Yorkshire streams would apply equally to all similar rivers.

"In view of these presentations it was therefore decided to alter the title to 'North-Country Flies,' the text remaining identical with that of the first edition."

Only 200 copies of the first edition were printed. I have never seen a copy, nor have I ever seen one advertised. When I received my copy of the latter edition, I read every word of it the first day I received it. And I marveled at the eleven plates of hand-painted soft hackles (see color plates) comprising 62 different patterns. I thought: "old Pritt is going to tell me how he and his Yorkshire brethren fished their flies." I was mistaken. Pritt's excuse was in his introduction. "It is not the purpose of this book to attempt to teach the art of fly fishing; the reader probably knows that experience is the only good master, though something of the fisherman's knowledge comes intuitively, and where the keen eye of one man will pick out the likely spots in a rippling stream, and see the quick rise of a trout, a hundred others will miss them, because, as the great father of fishers said, 'Angling is somewhat like poetry, man is to be born so.'

". . . . On the great questions of fishing up, across, or down stream it is useless to enter; everything depends upon the size of the river, the condition of the water, and the nature of the bait. To fish upstream is an unnecessary labour in a discoloured water, and to fish down stream in a clear water is to court both disappointment and ridicule; for, in the latter case, except in a turbulent eddy or a broken rapid, the angler will be perfectly visible to every fish for many a yard below him.

". . . . Then again, experience teaches that an angler need never despair of sport whatever quarter the wind may blow from, so long as it blows upstream; an upstream wind serves even a more important purpose than the provision of a ripple, —it keeps the feed on, and so long as there is food upon the water trout are on the look-out for it. If therefore you have your choice of two lengths of river up one of which a steady wind is blowing whilst the other fails to catch it, always take the one with the wind upon it. For the same reasons cast your flies as much as possible to that side of the river towards which the wind blows; the natural insects are blown thither and the trout are there. So too are trout collected under accumulations of froth; their instinct tells them it is a trap for flies and it is worth fishing. A trout will sometimes take any fly that is presented to him, but it is as well to remember that in nine cases out of ten he will not look at anything but the fly which is on the water so long as the rise is on."

There is not much there to hang a soft-hackled fly system on. But Pritt redeems himself by giving us, in the same introductory, his reasons for the excellent taking qualities of soft hackles.

"In one important matter of the fancy of Yorkshire anglers, and indeed of anglers all over the north of England, has undergone a change during the past twenty-five years. It is now conceded that a fly dressed hacklewise is generally to be preferred to a winged imitation. It is far more difficult to imitate a perfect insect and to afterwards impart to it a semblance of life in or on the water, than it is to produce something which is sufficiently near a resemblance of an imperfectly developed insect, struggling to attain the surface of the stream. Trout undoubtedly take a hackled fly for the insect just rising from the pupa in a half-drowned state; and the opening and closing of the fibres of the feathers give it an appearance of vitality, which even the most dexterous fly fisher will fail to impart to the winged imitation. Moreover, trout are not accustomed to seeing perfect winged flies underneath the surface of the water; a drowned fly always looks drowned, and although hungry trout will sometimes take a winged fly very well, it will generally be found that the hackled flies account for the largest number of fish. Perhaps too much attention is commonly given to the wings of artificial flies, and too little to the bodies.

". . . . Within reasonable limits, the flies for Yorkshire rivers, and for most other rivers of equal size,—for as the size of your river increases so, to a small extent, must your flies—cannot well be dressed too sparingly in the matter of feather. It stands to sense that to a creature with such wonderful vision as a trout it is better to err in offering a deception rather too small than too large.

". . . . It only remains to be said that the illustrations on the following plates have been very carefully copied from flies dressed by various Yorkshire makers. The originals, or others like them, have done service on half the rivers and lakes of England and Scotland, and have never failed to give a satisfactory account of themselves despite the lugubrious warnings of local hands that 'they were no use there.' You will be told this probably on every new river visited; yet may you safely fish your own flies and laugh to scorn the dismal prophecies of anglers who believe that the trout in their own river differ in their choice of flies from those of any other river in the universe."

Chapter II:

Pritt's Patterns

Following his introduction, Pritt goes directly into the descriptions of the flies. Hook sizes are different from the ones we use now. In Pritt's time, hook sizes were called "new." The hook sizes we use now are called "old." The following table will translate them to the standard sizes of today:

000	00	0	1	2	3	4	5	6	7	8	9
17	16	15	14	13	12	11	10	9	8	7	6

All of the descriptions and comments including the brief note on the seasons belong to Pritt. I have added the name of the order the artificial is supposed to imitate in parentheses following the hook size. This information comes from Edmonds and Lee and is not complete for the 62 patterns. I have decided to place all of the "Bloa" patterns in the order of the mayfly, for reasons also explained later. And I have deduced the orders of some of the other patterns by studying Edmonds and Lee's list and by comparing the materials of the known patterns to the unknown ones. For clarification, Edmonds and Lee's names of orders are followed by E. L.; mine are followed by S. N. Capitalization, punctuation and spelling follow Pritt verbatim. The original 11 color plates will be found in the color section of this book.

(The seasons are given approximately, the actual time of the appearance and disappearance of each fly being dependent on the mildness of the previous winter and the prevailing spring weather.)

Flies on Plate 1.
No. 1. Water Cricket. Hook No. 1
Wings.—Hackled with a feather from the Golden Plover's breast, in its summer plumage, or the wing or back of a Starling.
Body.—Yellow or Orange silk. It is sometimes ribbed with black silk.

In its early stages the insect of which this is supposed to be an imitation, is not a fly, but an active little spider. It runs upon the surface of the water, and is often taken greedily. The dressing shown in the plate is ample.

No. 2. Little Black. Hook 0, short. (Diptera, E. L.)
Wings.—Hackled with a feather from a Black Cock's hackle or Starling's neck.
Body.—Purple silk, dubbed sparingly with Magpie herl.
Head.—Purple.

This fly will will kill quite as well as No. 1. On very cold dull days in March and April, and again in August and September it will be found very useful. I have used it with great

effect on Ullswater. For the latter part of the season the following (not shown on the plate) is often used:
Wings.—Hackled with a feather from the outside of a Green Plover's wing, or a Swift's back.
Body.—Black silk, sparely dubbed with black Ostrich herl.

No. 3. Winter Brown. Hook 2. (Perlidae, E. L.)
Wings.—Hackled with a feather from the inside of a Woodcock's wing.
Body.—Orange silk—not too bright.
Head.—Peacock herl.

A favourite early fly on all the Yorkshire rivers, killing well on wild, windy days in March and April. The wings assume a lighter shade in the course of ten days after its first appearance on the water, when it is commonly dressed as No. 4.

No. 4. Little Winter Brown; or, Light Woodcock. Hook 1.
Wings.—Hackled with a feather from the outside of a Woodcock's wing.
Body.—Orange silk, with a spare dubbing of Hare's ear. Jackson recommends for the later dressing a feather from a hen pheasant's wing, but the above is quite as good.

No. 5. Brown Owl. Hook 1. (Trichoptera, E. L.)
Wings.—Hackled with a reddish feather from the outside of a Brown Owl's wing.
Body.—Orange silk.
Head.—Peacock herl.

This is a capital killer and may be safely fished all the year round, dressed a triffle smaller as the season advances.

No. 6. Fieldfare Bloa. Hook 1. (Ephemeridae, S. N.)

Wings.—From the bloa feather on a Fieldfare's rump, or failing that from the Tern, Bluetail, or Jay.
Body.—Yellow silk.
Legs.—From a feather from the Golden Plover.

Kills well during the latter part of March, and throughout April and May on rather warm days, with a wind. A favourite fly in Lancashire.

Flies on Plate 2.
No. 7. Dark Moor-game, or Orange Grouse, or Freckled Dun. Hook 0.
Wings.—Hackled with a black and orange feather from the Red Grouse, the hen bird for preference.
Body.—Orange silk.
Head.—Either orange silk, or Peacock herl.

A good fly during March and April, particularly in a brown water, when the river is clearing after a flood.

No. 8. Water-Hen Bloa. Hook 1. (Ephemeridae, E. L.)
Wings.—Hackled feather from the inside of a Water-Hen's wing.
Body.—Yellow silk, dubbed with the fur of the Water-rat.

This fly is identical with the blue dun of Ronalds, and is indispensable during March and April, and again towards the latter end of the season. It is also a useful grayling fly all through the winter months. No. 9 on the plate is another dressing of the same fly, and is a favourite in Upper Wharfedale. The hackled fly is, perhaps, preferable, as the real fly hatches out mainly on cold, windy days. If the day be warm the insect takes flight immediately on reaching the surface of the water; but if, as is commonly the case, the day is cold, it lingers on the surface, not completely hatched into perfect form, and is thus easily **pounced upon by expectant trout.**

No. 9. Dark Bloa. Hook 1. (Ephemeridae, E. L.)
Wings.—From the Starling's quill.
Body.—Dark claret silk.
Legs.—From black feather of a black Hen's neck.

Jackson dresses this fly somewhat similarly, and adds a tail as in the real insect. It is identical with one well-known and valued in the north as Broughton's Point.

No. 10. Dark Snipe. Hook 1. (Ephemeridae, E. L.)
Wings.—Hackled with a feather from the outside of a Snipe's wing.
Body.—Purple silk.

A splendid killer on cold days in the early part of the season, and is a favourite on the Ribble. In some districts it is not dressed until June, but the angler will find it too good to be neglected as a spring fly.

Flies on Plate 3.

March Browns *(Great Brown, Brown Drake, Dun Drake.)* **(Ephemeridae, E. L.)**

No. 11. Hook 3.
Wings.—From the tail of a Partridge.
Body.—Pale orange silk, dubbed with a little Hare's ear and yellow mohair, mixed; ribbed over with a little yellow silk.
Tail.—Forked with two strands from a Partridge's tail.
Legs.—From the back of a Partridge.

No. 12, Hook 2.
Wings.—From a quill feather of a Hen Pheasant.
Body, Tail, and Legs as in No. 11.

No. 13. Hook 2.
Wings.—Hackled with a reddish feather from the outside of a Woodcock's wing.
Body.—Orange silk, dubbed over with a little fur from a Fox's ear.

No. 14. Hook 2.
Wings.—From the tail of a Partridge.
Body.—Orange and yellow silk twisted, dubbed with fur from a Fox's ear.
Legs.—From a Wren's tail

No. 15. Hook 2.
Wings.—From the Hen Pheasant's wing.
Body and legs.—Same as in No. 14

The five dressings here given admit of little preference as killers. The hackled fly—though comparatively rarely dressed—will be found very useful on cold, rough days, and the winged flies are indispensable on fair days through March and April, and not infrequently into May. The female of the natural fly is a little lighter in the wing than the male, and a gradual change in the same direction appears to take place in the colour of all the flies as the season advances. Nos. 12 and 15 will therefore be useful later on, although if there is a heavy rise of the natural fly you will do well to have both the male and female fly on. Many anglers fish the March Brown, or a variation of it, more or less, all the year round, lessening the size as the months go on, and dressing it with a lighter feather, either from the grey goose or the hen pheasant. I have met many fishermen who believe that the fly which is often very abundant about the end of July or the beginning of August is in reality a second hatch of the March Brown. It is rather less and lighter in colour than the earlier hatchings, and like the latter changes to a red spinner. Jackson treats the later fly as an independent specimen, which he calls the August Brown, for which he gives a dressing almost identical with those I have quoted. Ronalds calls it the August Dun. No. 11 is a very excellent fly, and I have proved its killing properties not only on the Yorkshire rivers, but on the English and Scottish lakes, and notably on Loch Leven.

Flies on Plate 4.

No. 16. Red Clock or Pheasant. Hook 1.
Wings.—Hackled with a golden feather from a Cock Pheasant's neck, or from a small red cock's feather.
Body.—Yellow silk, with a twist of Peacock herl next the hackle.
Head.—Peacock herl.

Kills well sometimes on bright days in March and April.

No. 17. Red Palmer. Hook 1.
Body.—Green herl from Peacock, with a red cock's hackle wrapped over it.

This fly is best in a water which is fining after a flood, and occasionally it will be found very useful in a low clear river. I don't think it is a general favourite in Yorkshire, and it is only given because, whilst it will sometimes kill trout fairly, it is an excellent general grayling fly.

No. 18. Little Dark Watchet *(Iron Blue Dun.)* **Hook 0 short. (Ephemeridae, E. L.)**

Wings.—Hackled with a feather from a Jackdaw's neck, or outside a Coot's wing.
Body.—Orange and purple silk twisted, dubbed with down from a Water-rat.
Head.—Orange.

No. 19. Hook 0 short.
Wings.—From a Water-hen.
Body.—As in 18.
Head.—Ditto.
Legs.—From a Coot.

No. 20. Hook 0.
Wings.—From the breast of a Water-hen.
Body.—Orange silk dubbed with Mole's fur.
Head.—Orange
Legs.—A dirty whitish brown from a Hen's neck, or hairs from a Calf's tail, dyed yellow.

No. 21. Hook 0.
Wings.—Hackled with a feather from a Water-hen's breast; or, if you can get it, from a feather from a Bluecap for preference.
Body.—Orange silk, dubbed with Mole's fur.
Head.—Orange.

Four dressings, varying little, but by different makers. No. 20 is a fanciful imitation of the natural insect, but it is an excellent killer.

This is a famous fly, and is known on most English rivers, and by a great variety of names—the iron blue dun, iron blue drake, little iron blue, little water-hen, little dark dun &c. Jackson calls it the pigeon blue bloa. In his "Book on Angling,"

Mr. Francis overlooks it in Jackson, and says, "Jackson does not give this fly till June, though all other authors introduce it in April." It is No. 14 on Jackson's plates, Mr. Francis having mistaken No. 39 for it. Jackson gives the dressing for his No. 14, almost identically with No. 20 as above, except that he adds the tail. On the Eden it is dressed from the breast of the cock Water-hen.

The natural fly appears on the Yorkshire rivers about the same time as the swallows first come, and the artificial fly will often kill well on cold days throughout the season. The real fly comes out in vast numbers with any glint of sunshine from the middle of April to the end of May, and whilst it is on, trout commonly prefer it to anything else. It is a very perfect little insect, and very beautiful to look at when it reaches the surface of the water, newly hatched. The male fly has a distinct crown of orange, or brownish red, which is also visible in the female, though not to any equal extent. The dark watchet is one of the daintiest morsels with which you can tempt a trout, and one of the most difficult to imitate satisfactorily.

Flies on Plate 5.

No. 22. Dark Spanish Needle *(Needle Brown).* **Hook 0. (Perlidae, E. L.)**

Wings.—Hackled with a feather from the darkest part of a Brown Owl's wing.
Body.—Orange silk.
Head.—Peacock herl.

A good standard fly all through the season; but the natural insect cannot be imitated as a winged fly with any approach to a similitude to nature, owing to its diminutive size and the peculiar situation of its wings. Trout will often take it when few other flies will kill; the natural fly is most plentiful on the water on days with flying clouds and fitful bursts of sunshine, with a cold wind blowing underneath. Ronalds does not mention it. It is, however, a favourite in Yorkshire, particularly on the Rye, the Ure, and the Wharfe. It is often a capital killer on damp, close days in September, and will be found very useful as a grayling fly as far on as the beginning of December. The name 'Needle' was probably given to it owing to the peculiar steely shade visible on the wings.

No. 23. Light Spanish Needle. Hook 0. (Perlidae, E. L.)
Wings.—Hackled with a feather from inside a Jack-Snipe's wing, or from the breast of a young Starling.
Body.—Crimson silk.
Head.—Peacock herl.

Another form of No. 22, more suitable for warm days. The shades of the natural flies vary considerably.

No. 24. Light Watchet *(Spinning Jenny; Pearl Drake.)* **Hook 0. (Ephemeridae, S. N.)**
Wings.—From the Jay.
Body.—Straw coloured silk.
Legs.—Fibres from a yellow Plover.

This is not a good fly to imitate. It is the metamorphosis of the dark watchet or iron blue dun, and both are often on the water together. Jackson calls it the little white spinner. It is a very delicate transparent insect, and most authorities are content to give a general instruction to dress it from the lightest dun hackle you can get. Most fly-dressers make some attempt to imitate the variations of colour in the extremities of the body of the natural insect, but the figure on the plate will kill well enough when trout are in the humour. Mr. Walbran

COLOR PLATES

Pritt: The first 11 pages were shot as they appeared in Pritt's book, "North-Country Flies." They show the 62 patterns described in the text.

Edmonds and Lee: The 12th color page was shot from Edmonds and Lee's book, "Brook and River Trouting." The color plate illustrates the authors' attempts to show the hackles, fur and herls used in the fly patterns.

The 13th color page is of natural and dyed body hackles. Top row: Three partridge hackles from the same skin, grouse hackle. Second row: Starling, jackdaw, pheasant and woodcock. Third row: Dyed partridge hackles. Fourth row: Natural hen body hackles.

The 14th color page is of feathers from wings of various birds, herls and furs. Top row: Waterhen, woodcock, jackdaw, starling, snipe, grouse and golden plover. Second row: Golden pheasant rooster herls, pheasant herls, natural peacock herls, heron herls and dyed peacock herls. Bottom row: Fur from mole, hare's face and tup's fur.

The 15th color page is of the 20 soft hackles currently used by the author and other addicts. The order is left to right. Top row: Snipe and purple, tup's indispensable, partridge and orange, grouse and orange, partridge and green and fur thorax. Second row: Partridge and yellow, starling and herl, partridge and yellow and fur thorax, iron blue dun, Dean's black. Third row: Brown drake, black and red dun, pheasant tail, Cumberland, partridge and green. Fourth row: Snipe and yellow, pheasant tail with fur thorax, March brown spider, partridge and orange and fur thorax, golden pheasant tail with fur thorax.

NORTH COUNTRY TROUT FLIES.

PLATE 1. MARCH.

Nº 1. WATER CRICKET.

Nº 2. LITTLE BLACK.

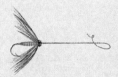

Nº 3. WINTER BROWN.

Nº 4. LITTLE WINTER BROWN
OR LIGHT WOODCOCK.

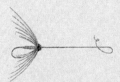

Nº 5. BROWN OWL.

Nº 6. FIELDFARE BLOA.

Mintern Bros. lith.

NORTH COUNTRY TROUT FLIES.

PLATE 2. MARCH.

Nº 7. DARK MOORGAME
OR ORANGE GROUSE.

Nº 8. WATERHEN BLOA.

Nº 9. DARK BLOA.

Nº 10. DARK SNIPE.

NORTH COUNTRY TROUT FLIES.

PLATE 3.   MARCH

Nº 11.   Nº 12.

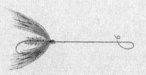

Nº 13.

Nº 14.   Nº 15.

MARCH BROWNS.

NORTH COUNTRY TROUT FLIES.

PLATE 4.   MARCH & APRIL.

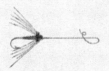

Nº 16. RED CLOCK OR PHEASANT.

Nº 17. RED PALMER.

Nº 18.

Nº 19.

Nº 20.

Nº 21.

Nºs 18, 19, 20 & 21, FOUR DRESSINGS OF THE LITTLE DARK WATCHET OR IRON BLUE DUN.

NORTH COUNTRY TROUT FLIES.

PLATE 5.   MARCH & APRIL.

Nº 22. DARK SPANISH NEEDLE.   Nº 23 LIGHT SPANISH NEEDLE

Nº 24. LIGHT WATCHET.

Nº 25.   Nº 26.
Nºs 25 & 26. OLIVE BLOAS.

NORTH COUNTRY TROUT FLIES.

PLATE 6. APRIL.

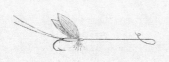

Nº 27. YELLOW LEGG'D BLOA.

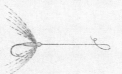

Nº 28. YELLOW PARTRIDGE.

Nº 29. SNIPE BLOA.

Nº 30. SNIPE BLOA.

Nº 31. BROWN WATCHET.

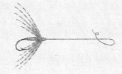

Nº 32. ORANGE PARTRIDGE.

NORTH COUNTRY TROUT FLIES.

PLATE 7.   APRIL.

Nº 33. GREENTAIL.

Nº 34. SANDFLY.

Nº 35. DOTTEREL.

Nº 36. YELLOW SALLY.

Nº 37. POULT BLOA.   OR

Nº 38. LIGHT BLOA.

NORTH COUNTRY TROUT FLIES.

PLATE 8. APRIL & MAY.

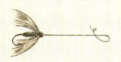

Nº 39. OLD MASTER.

Nº 40. STONE MIDGE.

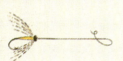

Nº 41. GREY MIDGE.

Nº 42. KNOTTED MIDGE.

Nº 43. SANDY MOORGAME.

Nº 44. BLUE PARTRIDGE.

NORTH COUNTRY TROUT FLIES.

PLATE 9. MAY & JUNE.

Nº 45. RED OWL.

Nº 46. STONE BLOA.

Nº 47. SMALL BLUE BLOA.

Nº 48. GREENSLEEVES.

Nº 49. THORNFLY DUN.

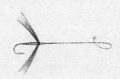

Nº 50. CURLEW.

NORTH COUNTRY TROUT FLIES.

PLATE 10.   JUNE & JULY.

Nº 51. STARLING BLOA.

Nº 52. SMALL ANT.

Nº 53. FOG BLACK.

Nº 54. CUBDOWN BLOA.

Nº 55. CINNAMON.

Nº 56. SMOKE FLY.

NORTH COUNTRY TROUT FLIES.

PLATE 11.   JUNE & JULY.

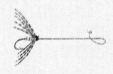

Nº 57. GREY PARTRIDGE.

Nº 58. LARGE ANT.

Nº 59. SEA SWALLOW.

Nº 60. JULY DUN.

Nº 61. BLACK GNAT.

Nº 62. BLACK SNIPE.

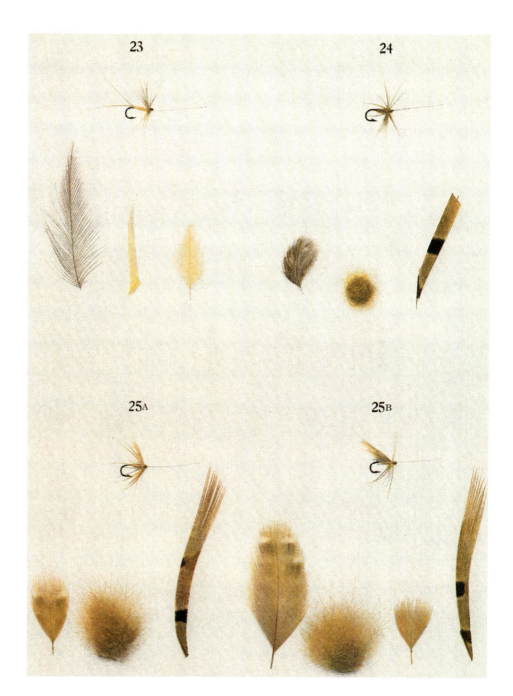

remarks, in his "Notes" to Theakston, that he has never found the artificial fly kill well, and I know one fly-maker in the county who has ceased to dress it, in something like despair at his inability to produce an imitation of the natural fly to his satisfaction. It should be fished on mild days and in the evening during summer.

No. 25. Olive Bloa. Hook 1. (Ephemeridae, E. L.)
Wings.—From a Starling's quill.
Body.—Greenish yellow silk.
Legs.—White hackle from a Hen's neck, stained to olive in onions.

No. 26. Olive Bloa. Hook 0. (Ephemeridae, E. L.)
Wings.—Hackled with a feather from a Lapwing's back or rump.
Body.—Yellow silk.
Head.—Orange silk.

Known by a great variety of names, and always useful. Either of the forms here given will kill well on cold, windy days, particularly about midday in March and April.

Flies on Plate 6.

No. 27. Yellow-Legged Bloa *(Yellow Dun.)* **Hook 1. (Ephemeridae, E. L.)**
Wings.—From a young Starling's quill feather.
Body.—Yellow silk, waxed well, so as to make it nearly olive.
Legs.—Ginger hackle from a Cochin-China Hen's neck.
Tail: Two strands of the above.

A first-rate killer, indispensable during its season.

No. 28. Yellow Partridge *(Grey Gnat.)* **Hook 1. (Perlidae and Diptera, E. L.)**
Wings.—Hackled with a light feather from the back of a Partridge.
Body.—Yellow silk.

A good killer almost any time during April.

No. 29. Snipe Bloa. Hook 1. (Ephemeridae, E. L.)
Wings.—Hackled with a feather from the inside of a Jack Snipe's wing.
Body: Straw-coloured silk.

No. 30. Snipe Bloa. Hook 0. (Ephemeridae, S. N.)
Wings.—Hackled with a feather from under the Snipe's wing.
Body.—Yellow silk, with a spare dubbing of Mole's fur, but not sufficient to hide the yellow body.

Two dressings of the same fly, and practically identical. It is a splendid killer, and many anglers fish it more or less all the year round. It is Theakston's Bloa brown, and is probably to be identified with the Light Bloa of Jackson. It is fished universally in Yorkshire and Lancashire, and it will account for its share of fish at any time, and particularly on cold, wild days, all through the season.

No. 31. Brown Watchet *(Little Brown Dun.)* **Hook 1. (Ephemeridae, S. N.)**
Wings.—Hackled with a well dappled feather from a Partridge's back.
Body.—Orange silk.
Head.—Peacock herl.

**No. 32. Orange Partridge. Hook 1. (Perlidae and Ephemeridae,

E. L.)
Wings.—Hackled as in No. 31.
Body.—Orange silk.

These are practically the same flies, and are very excellent killers. I prefer the dressing of No. 32 myself, although one will kill as well as the other, and the angler may look upon one of them as indispensable on his cast from April to September, on warm days. It is the Turkey Brown of Ronalds, and the Spiral Brown Drake of Theakston.

Flies on Plate 7.

No. 33. Greentail *(Grannom Fly.)* **Hook 1. (Trichoptera, S. N.)**
Wings.—Hackled with a feather from the inside of a Woodcock's wing, or from a Partridge's neck, or from under a Hen Pheasant's wing.
Body.—Lead coloured silk, twisted with a little fur from a Hare's face.
Tail.—Green silk, wrapped over the lower part of the body.

This fly does not last very long, and appears to be quite extinct for the season in about eighteen days after its first appearance on the water. It is not always to be relied on as a killer, although, now and then, trout will make a dead set at it, and take nothing else. It kills best in the morning and evening, on warm days.

No. 34. Sandfly. Hook 1.
Wings.—From a sandy feather from a Landrail's wing.
Body.—Light brown silk, ribbed with sandy fur from a Hare.
Legs.—Dark ginger hackle.

This fly is commonly dressed rather large in the wing. It will not always kill. It does best in warm, gloomy weather, and sometimes with a moderate wind blowing on a dub it will be found useful. It is a favourite on the Ribble, where it is often taken well.

No. 35. Dotterel. Hook 1. (Ephemeridae, E. L.)
Wings.—Hackled with a feather from the outside of a male Dotterel's wing.
Body.—Straw-coloured silk; some anglers prefer Orange silk.
Head.—Straw-coloured, or orange silk.

This fly is undoubtedly a splendid killer, although it may be questioned whether its reputation on all the Yorkshire, and other north country rivers, is not in excess of its merits. As a matter of fact a feather from a young curlew will be found equally attractive to the trout. The dotterel is a good standard fly all through the season from the end of April, more especially on rather cold days.

No. 36. Yellow Sally. Hook 0.
Wings.—From a Green Linnet's tail.
Body.—Yellow silk.
Legs.—White feather from a Hen's neck, dyed yellow in onions.

This fly is dressed on almost every Yorkshire river, and it is therefore included, but it rarely kills well, and the natural insect does not appear to be much relished by trout.

Nos. 37 & 38. Poult Bloa, or Light Bloa. Hook 0. (Ephemeridae, E. L.)
Wings.—Hackled with a feather from under the wing of a young Grouse.
Body.—Light yellow silk.

A fair killer on cold days all through the season. For warm days a fancy dressing of it, as under, will sometimes be found useful:—Wings, hackled as above; Body, straw-coloured silk, with a twist of purple silk around it; and a peacock herl head.

Flies on Plate 8.
No. 39. Old Master. Hook 1. (Ephemeridae, E. L.)
Wings.—Hackled with a feather from the inside of a Woodcock's wing.
Body.—Ash-coloured silk, wrapped over with Heron's herl.

This is a capital killer from April to the end of August, on warm days, or in the evenings. It was originally dressed by Bradley, of Otley, and in his time he caught many heavy dishes of trout with it. It bears some resemblance to "Greenwell's Glory."

No. 40. Stone Midge. Hook 0. (Diptera, E. L.)
Wings.—Hackled with a feather from a Pewit's neck, breast or rump.
Body.—Ash-coloured silk, dubbed sparely with Heron's herl.
Head.—Magpie herl.

The natural fly is not good to imitate owing to its diminutive size, but the above will kill well on cool days.

No. 41. Grey Midge. Hook 0. (Diptera, S. N.)
Wings.—Hackled with a feather from a Woodcock's breast.
Body.—Yellow silk.
Head.—Peacock herl.

Kills best on warm days, and summer evenings.

No. 42. Knotted Midge. Hook 0. (Diptera, E. L.)
Wings.—Hackled with a feather from the back of a Swift or Martin, or from the shoulder of a Pewit's wing.
Body.—Ash-coloured silk, dubbed with Heron's herl, rather

more fully than in No. 40.
Head.—Magpie herl.

Does very well sometimes on hot stuffy days, when thunder is about.

No. 43. Sandy Moorgame. Hook 0. (Ephemeridae, S. N.)
Wings.—Hackled with a dark, reddish-brown feather from the back of a Grouse.
Body.—Dark brown silk.
Head.—Ditto.

This is a very useful fly from May to the end of July, and it is not to be neglected in a brown water clearing after a flood. It is probably identical with the dark dun of Theakston.

No. 44. Blue Partridge. Hook 1. (Diptera, E. L.)
Wings.—Hackled with a feather from a Partridge's back.
Body.—Blue silk dubbed with a little lead-coloured lamb's wool.

A first-rate killer in a biggish water anytime after the middle of May.

Flies on Plate 9.

No. 45. Red Owl (*Brown Dun.*) **Hook 1. (Ephemeridae, S. N.)**
Wings.—Hackled with a red feather from a Brown Owl's wing; shorter in the fibre than that used for No. 5.
Body.—Orange silk.
Head.—Peacock herl.

A good killer in warm weather, particularly in the evening.

No. 46. Stone Bloa. Hook 0. (Ephemeridae, S. N.)
Wings.—From a feather from under a Jack Snipe's wing.
Body.—Yellow silk.

Legs.—Fibres from a Jack Snipe's feather.

This fly is useful from the beginning of June until the end of the season; it kills well occasionally about mid-day, but is best as an evening fly.

No. 47. Small Blue Bloa. Hook 0. (Ephemeridae, S. N.)
Wings.—From a feather from a Bluecap's tail.
Body.—Orange silk.
Legs.—Pale yellow fibres.

I have been unable to identify this with any fly dressed by Jackson, Ronalds, Theakston, or others. Most of them give flies of almost similar names, and all of them differ greatly in the dressing. The fly here given will be found a good, all-around summer killer.

No. 48. Greensleeves. Hook. 1. (Ephemeridae, S. N.)
Wings.—Hackled with a feather from the inside of a Woodcock's wing or from a hen Pheasant's neck.
Body.—Bright green silk.
Head.—Ditto

Another form of Ronald's "Gold-eyed gauze wing," useful only on dull, sultry days, and occasionally in the evening. Not generally dressed, but will now and then kill fairly.

No. 49. Thornfly Dun. Hook 1.
Wings.—Hackled with a Landrail's feather, taken from under the wing.
Body.—Orange silk.
Head.—Peacock herl.

A very excellent fly in a good bold brown water on warm days in summer, from June onwards. It is a variation of No. 5, and equally useful. Dressed with a redder feather it is the same fly as that known as Blacker's Red.

No. 50. Curlew, Hook 0.
Wings.—Hackled with a small feather from the outside of a young Curlew's wing (August at the latest).
Body.—Orange silk for preference, but maroon or yellow will sometimes kill equally well.

The pattern for this fly was supplied to me by Mr. Henry Cadman, of Gomersal, who has dressed it for a good many seasons past. It will kill almost at anytime, and particularly in a rather low and clear river. A feather from a Green Plover will kill, but the Curlew is better and should be used in preference.

Flies on Plate 10.

No. 51. Starling Bloa. Hook 0. (Ephemeridae, S. N.)
Wings.—Hackled, with the lightest feather from a young Starling's wing.
Body.—Straw-coloured silk. Some anglers prefer white silk.

Probably Jackson's "Nankeen Spinner." It will kill on cold days in May, and late in the evenings in June and July.

No. 52. Small Ant. Hook 0.
Wings.—Hackled with a feather from a Tomtit's tail.
Body and Head.—A bright brownish Peacock's herl; body dressed full, as shown in the plate.

Is best on hot days in July and August. The natural fly is abundant on almost every English river, and the artificial fly is alluded to by most writers. It will now and then do great execution, particularly after a flight of ants.

No. 53. Fog Black. Hook 0.

Wings.—From a Bullfinch's wing.
Body.—Dark purple silk, dubbed with a dark Heron's herl, or, more sparingly, with black Ostrich herl.
Legs.—From the Starling's neck.

Suitable for cold dark days, from June to the end of the season. The natural fly is very diminutive, and the artificial must be kept as small as possible. A capital grayling fly.

No. 54. Cubdown Bloa. Hook 1. (Ephemeridae, E. L.)
Wings.—From the inside of a Swift's wing, or from a Lapwing's apron.
Body.—Yellow silk, dubbed with down from a Fox cub, or fur from a Water-rat.
Legs.—From a Plover's feather.

Useful towards evening through June and July.

No. 55. Cinnamon. Hook 1.
Wings.—Hackled with a feather from a Brown Owl's wing.
Body.—Yellow silk, dubbed with fur from a Water-rat.
Head.—Peacock herl.

A capital summer fly, particularly in the evening. It is well known, and universally fished during July and August, in Yorkshire and Lancashire. Jackson says it is best taken in a shower.

No. 56. Smoke Fly. Hook 1.
Wings.—Hackled (as in the plate) with a feather from a young Grouse.
Body.—Bright brown Peacock's herl. It is sometimes dressed with a twist of silver round the body.

More or less a fancy fly, and will only kill in certain curious states of the weather and the water. On sluggish water, in dull, heavy, sultry weather, it is sometimes useful.

Flies on Plate 11.

No. 57. Grey Partridge *(Grey Watchet.)* **Hook 0.**
Wings.—Hackled with a light feather from a Partridge's breast.
Body.—Straw-coloured silk.
Head.—Peacock herl.

For cold days, and in the evenings during June and July.

No. 58. Large Ant. Hook 0.
Wings.—From a Starling's quill.
Body.—Orange silk wrapped over the lower part, with three turns of a copper-coloured Peacock's herl, as shown in the plate.
Head.—Peacock's herl.
Legs.—Fibres from the light part of a Starling's quill feather.

Kills best on warm days towards the latter part of the season. It is identical with Jackson's "Orange Stinger." The natural fly never appears in large numbers.

No. 59. Sea Swallow. Hook 0.
Wings.—From a very light feather from the outside of a Sea Swallow's wing.
Body.—White silk.
Legs.—Fibres from the wing feathers.

Mainly an evening fly.

No. 60. July Dun. Hook 1. (Ephemeridae, E. L.)
Wings.—From a Starling's quill.
Body.—Yellow silk dubbed with a little Mole's fur.
Legs.—Fibre from a bluish dun Hen's neck.

This is probably Jackson's little Olive bloa, and is perhaps the same fly as Theakston's pale blue Drake. It is common on most English rivers, and trout will occasionally take it with great avidity.

No. 61. Black Gnat. Hook 0. Short. (Diptera, E. L.)
Wings.—None.
Body.—A little Ostrich herl.

The diminutive size of the natural insect and the consequent difficulty in imitating it, is probably only one reason why anglers universally lament their inability to catch trout whilst the black gnat is on. As a matter of fact you may try trout with anything you like, but they will rarely be diverted from the natural fly. The specimen here given will kill as well as any other imitation, and it is quite big enough and sufficiently like a hackle imitation of the fly, without any attempt to add the wings.

No. 62. Black Snipe. Hook 0.
Wings.—Hackled with a Jack Snipe's feather from under the wing.
Body.—Dark green Peacock herl.

This is an old Yorkshire fly, quoted in many manuscripts on angling, still in existence, although it is not generally dressed. It will kill well almost all the year round, and my own experience has proved it is a good general fly.

Chapter III:

Pritt on Fishing, and the Case of the Bloas

These excerpts and the patterns from "North-Country Flies," are all that is important to the American soft-hackled fly addict. As there was no clear method of fishing outlined in the book, so was there no method of tying outlined in it. And as you will notice from the color plates, all the flies were tied on silkworm gut, a practice which persisted, at least for wet flies, long after eyed hooks were commonly available.

A "splendid killer," "kills well," "will kill," and "capital killer," are frightening and perhaps misleading descriptions of many of the 62 patterns by today's catch-and-release American standards. In Pritt's time and even today in England and Europe, practically every trout over seven or eight inches was and is killed. If a fly or a group of flies became known for their effectiveness, they became "killers," like the Alexandra and Butcher which were supposedly outlawed on some rivers because of their effectiveness.

When I fished the Test during the mid-forties, I was told by the river keeper to kill all fish, because "They won't rise to the artificial after they're once hooked." We know now that this is not true and never has been. The reason British and Scots killed fish then and still kill trout and salmon is that generally, they pay dearly for the right to fish the water.

As you read the description of Pritt's flies you must have noticed the repetitious use of the term, Bloa. Pritt used it to name 13 flies in the list such as "Water-hen Bloa, Dark Bloa, Fieldfare Bloa, Yellow-legged Bloa, etc." To confuse things a little further, he also uses it as an adjective, ". . . . from the bloa feather on a Fieldfare's rump." This use seems to imply a color. But looking at all of the illustrations of the bloa patterns, one does not find a similarity in color, except in the hackle.

The Oxford English Dictionary shows no definition for the word, by itself. But under the word, Blae, we find that Bloa is a form of that word. The broad definition of both is "dark blue or a dark color between black and blue." Other definitions are "livid, of a lighter shade such as bluish grey and lead colored." According to the dictionary, the word can also be used to describe the weather, as "bleak and sunless," or "grey as opposed to white; unbleached."

I wrote to a Yorkshire friend, Ivor Jones, and asked him to give me a definition. Here is his reply: "The word Bloa originates in the dales of Yorkshire and is not now used to my knowledge except by fly-tyers and fly fishermen." He quotes Courtney Williams' "Dictionary of Trout Flies." "Poult Bloa... an effective suggestion of the nymph of the Blue Winged Olive. It will take trout throughout the season especially on cold, dull days. Dressing: Body: Yellow silk dubbed with red squirrel. Hackled with the slate blue feather from the under wing of a young grouse." Then Ivor quotes John Swarbrick's "Wharfedale Flies," printed in 1807. "Bloa is a curious term. It is sometimes spelt 'Blo' or 'Bloo' but that may be because the gentlemen were somewhat illiterate. Its meaning is by no means clear and north-country men explain it in many divers ways, no two of which appear to agree."

Ivor goes on to quote one of Yorkshire's finest anglers, a J.H.R. Bazely. "It refers I think to the cold, cloudy, bleak sort of weather-feather used frequently with a yellow or partially yellow body. This is my conception of it and I may be wrong but I don't think so."

I also wrote a letter to the editors of "Trout and Salmon," a fine, English angling monthly, for further information on the term, Bloa. I was overwhelmed by the kind response of the magazine's readers. One gentleman sent me several bloa patterns, with a sparseness and delicacy which I had never seen before. Another sent typical bloa feathers from snipe, jackdaw and waterhen. Another angler quoted from "The Art of the Wet Fly," by W. S. Roger Fogg, who said, ". . .the name of the fly depicts the hackle."

This last quote cleared up something for me because, though the hackle colors in Pritt's bloas are basically a dusty, gray blue, and most of the bodies are yellow, there are in addition red-, green-, orange- and straw-colored bodies.

So much for the color. Now, let's try to figure out the insect order. Cross checking with the established insect orders of Edmonds and Lee in the next chapter, we find that the bloa patterns are for the most part mayflies. Courtney Williams' poult bloa was a mayfly, the blue-winged olive. The word, "unbleached," was also used as a synonym in the dictionary for bloa. And isn't this a pretty good description of the dusty, powdery wings of all mayfly duns? Let's rest on that: Bloa, a gray/blue-hackled fly with a light or dark body representing mayfly duns.

Another matter for discussion is the use of several different kinds of herls wrapped at the heads of many of the patterns. This practice is very intriguing because no American writer I know of has ever mentioned it.

Except for a couple of Yorkshire rivers, most of them are rocky and gravelly, which must, because of what we know about the Trichoptera, produce an abundance of flies of this order. Caddis pupae have fuzzy, enlarged heads. The local angler and fly tyer who first recognized this and tied on the first herl head to imitate it, was followed by others until the practice was routine on many flies, even those which did not try to imitate the caddis. I'll quote Ivor Jones again. "These could be, as you say, to imitate the caddis pupae. They could also imitate any hatching insect with the head emerging from the nymphal shuck. Herl fibres trap air."

For the last two years, I have tied soft hackles with these herl wrapped heads. I have used natural peacock, ostrich, and cock pheasant. The flies look very appetizing, and they "kill" trout as well as soft-hackled flies tied without them. And as Ivor says, there is the possibility that in the water, the fuzzy heads trap air and create mysterious bubbles, a phenomenon I noticed a few years ago when I was photographing the action of soft hackles in running water. The herls are very easy to tie. You will find a description of the method in the tying section of this book.

One other little confusion demands investigation. In his descriptions of the flies, Pritt often treats the artificial and the real insect as one and the same. His No. 3, for example, starts out as the Winter Brown. He says it kills well on wild, windy days in March and April. Suddenly, the artificial becomes the real insect when, "the wings assume a lighter shade in the course of ten days after its first appearance on the water, when it is commonly dressed as No. 4." In midstream, or midair, if you like, the artificial has become the real insect.

This is a tiny, literary objection. The fact remains that Pritt wrote well about angling. He was, during the time of the publication of "North-Country Flies," angling editor of the Yorkshire Post. Apparently he could draw, too, because the hand-painted illustrations in the book were done after his own drawings. The Yorkshire Post columns, many of which were published in his last book, "An Angler's Basket," 1896, are informational as well as humorous. There is no dogma. His descriptions of river and meadows and flora and fauna are vivid. English usage is good. And he shows a "local's" common sense approach to solving the problems of catching trout. Here are some examples from the last named book:

On big trout: "It was a reyt good trout; but what! that's two months sin', and it were three pund weight then; and what it's gotten to by this time, may be ye can reckon as weel as I can, for ye knaw a big fish is a thing 'at graws terble fast when it's once oot o' t' watter."

On nature: "The country is all like a garden, as Longfellow described England in his far-off western home. The hedgerows and the umbrageous lanes are fringed with lilacs and laburnums and wild flowers in profusion; the first fresh green of the reluctant spring is on every tree and every blade; acres of apple blossoms are around, and meadow-sweet and hawthorn scent the air; melodious birds are singing among the trembling leaves and in the sky, and white cascades divide deep pine-covered hill-sides, and are foaming and dashing and making merry music everywhere as they go to join the angler's playground—the river. Call the fisherman's sport dull, stupid, slow, if you will, but at least admit that no other sportsman ever sees nature or has time to see her at home and at her best, pure and unsullied by any of the blackening arts of man."

On the position of trout in streams: "The early spring-trout fisher usually finds himself at fault in his first efforts to find the fish at the beginning of each season. Their exact situation in the streams and dubs varies according to the prevailing temperature, atmospheric and aquatic. When trout return to the main river from the tributary becks after the spawning season, they are ill-conditioned and too weak to stem the force of a powerful current. They, therefore, find their first resting-places in the quiet dubs, and usually at the lower end of them, where the current is gentle. As the warmth of the sun increases with the advancing season, aquatic life begins to move from under the stones and about the rocks, gravel, and weeds, and the ravenous fish feed greedily on it, a few fine days at this period of the year having a remarkable effect in bringing trout into condition. Of course, the surface-food of trout, as all anglers know, is a mere fraction of the sustenance they require, and it is tolerably certain that a trout is at all times feeding on the minute atoms trundled along by the current or found by him in his foraging expeditions. As soon as the fish get a little stronger they move away from the quiet places in the dubs and come nearer to the rough streams, knowing very well that the rapid current is more likely to bring down abundance of food from the ground above."

On artificial flies: "Most fly-dressers fail to make really good flies because they put too much stuff on the hook rather than too little. Many of them, and this applies especially to the producers of London flies, have no knowledge of the living insect of which they are presumed to be making something of an imitation. An exact imitation of a fly, as every old fly-fisher knows, is quite unnecessary; but those who aim to dress flies accurately should certainly take the trouble to examine the living insect on the water, and learn something of its life-history."

On familiarity: "Most old anglers have observed that trout do not take all the natural dainties of the river for some days after their first appearance on the surface of the water. This is the case with all the different flies and the creeper also. Fish require to become familiar with their appearance before they take them greedily, just as, I dare say, you observed was the case with your wife in regard to oysters; but, having once acquired the taste, 'ma conscience' how they do go it!"

On first principles: "Two 'first principles' are necessary in angling: one to know where the fish are, the other to avoid letting them know where you are."

On color: "Do colours of different kinds present the same hues to the vision of fish as they do to our eyes? The merciful powers forbid that it should be otherwise, else what tommyrot some of us have written in our time about being careful to get that exact shade of feather and silk."

On caddis cases: ". . .have you ever in an idle or unsuccesful hour paused to examining the apparently unattractive cases in which the larvae of the phryganidae exist, the cases commonly known as caddis or stick baits? If you will condescend to such trifles you will be surprised to notice first of all that they differ; each kind of fly of this species builds a different kind of house, and Nature, with her usual liberality, has prepared surprises for those who care to look, even in these lowly insects. Here is one solidly constructed of bits of hard gravel, rough rock and shining sand, but within as smooth, and no doubt as easy to wear, as an old shoe; here is another, in which two or three long chips of weed form the strengthening props of the abode; and here another one (such as a number of us examined through a powerful magnifier on the noisy beck behind the hamlet of Howietown by Ullswater); it is composed of tiny atoms of coloured stone and spar, blue, amber, pink, green, red and brown set side by side in a truly wonderful way like Mosaic work, and held together by a thin transparent groundwork; held up to the light it is as pretty as anything you can fancy. If you will only take the trouble to look deeply into the surroundings of angling, you will find that every peep will teach you something worth knowing and remembering."

On the iron blue dun: "There is to my eye and my thinking, nothing in nature that it was ever yet my lot to see more wonderful, more amazing in its delicate loveliness than what the fly anglers call the 'iron blue dun,' just newly hatched from the depths of the cool river, and standing suddenly, as by a miracle, in all the glory of wings on the shining water. Look at it closely. Did you ever see such undefinable tissue, veined so tenderly and coloured so faintly, as you see in these wings—wings that even a rude breath will ruin? Look at the tiny body, perfect in shape and soft as velvet to the touch. Even at the bottom of the dark river Old Mother Nature has been busy putting golden rings around the insect and a crown of brilliant orange on his head, a flattering attention which she omits to pay his future wife."

And on trout's vision: "The eye of a trout is a wonderful evidence of the adaptation by nature of means to ends. The very smallest midge-fly that human skill can dress is often picked up by a trout out of a rough tumbling stream where an angler's feet can scarcely maintain a hold from the strength and speed of the water."

We all take a hero in fly fishing. He may be a literary figure who thinks as you do and who writes at the high, low, or middle-brow level which appeals to you. He may be the friendly old neighbor, who, having no boys of his own, adopts you as his piscatorial offspring, and from whom you inherit the desire, knowledge, and tradition.

Pritt is mine.

Chapter IV:

*Edmonds and Lee:
Matching
Artificials
to Naturals*

Thirty years passed between "North-Country Flies," and "Brook and River Trouting," privately printed by Edmonds and Lee, in 1916, in Bradford, Yorkshire. Edmonds was a textile manufacturer and Lee, a solicitor. One thousand copies were printed as standard, while a limited edition of 50 copies featuring 36 artificial flies tied by Hardy Bros. and including a selection of silks, was also put together. While the standard copy today is valued at around $150, the special edition is valued at around $2500. "Brook and River Trouting," has recently been reprinted from the original color plates and can be purchased from: The Orange Partridge Press, 59/61 East Parade, Ilkley, West Yorkshire, LS298JP, United Kingdom.

There are 36 patterns in "Brook and River Trouting," including two dry flies tied on eyed hooks. Of the remaining 34, all but 8 are directly from Pritt's list. Yet, his name is not mentioned once throughout the book.

The authors' aim was to produce "A Manual of Modern North Country Methods," which "not only prescribed the exact part of a bird from which the correct feathers should be taken, but illustrated such feathers and other materials (as also the flies made therefrom), in colour, would be a help, at least to beginners in the craft, and not merely an encumbrance on angling literature."

The 34 wet fly patterns are tied on silk gut, with the same sparseness recommended by Pritt and others before him. The authors recommend short hooks and short bodies with "the tail ends of the bodies not carried further down the hook than half way between the point of the hook and the point of the barb." The authors also recommend, as I have, using the same shade of silk for the heads and bodies. The two dry fly patterns are spinners tied on eyed hooks.

The authors give two methods of wet fly fishing, upstream and down. "The downstream method advocated might quite appropriately be termed across-stream fishing, as the angler faces the bank towards which he purposes fishing, casts across and slightly upstream, then allows the flies to be carried without drag till they reach a point a few yards below where they alighted upon the water. Wading downstream a yard or more, he repeats the cast, until the whole stream has been worked in this manner."

This is not the authors' preferred method. According to them it should be used only in big, strong, and full water; after the hatch; during evening fishing when the river flows toward sunset; or when a heavy downstream wind leaves the angler no choice.

On smaller streams and when a hatch is noticed, the upstream method is suggested. A very short line is used and the angler casts to a definite point, not necessarily to a rising fish. To help in controlling drag, he casts a wavy line, "as the current has to pick up the slack before the drag takes effect on the flies."

Continuing, according to Edmonds and Lee, the angler steps into the stream and begins to fish his side first. "Every cast is made to a definite point, not necessarily to a rising fish, as in dry-fly fishing, but successively to each of the many little runs, eddies, channels, and slack waters behind boulders, which his experience teaches are likely to hold feeding fish."

When the angler has exhausted his first position, he steps further into the stream and repeats his casting, the first nearly straight above, then at greater angles and lengthening his line to reach the likely positions further out.

"To fish a stream or length of river systematically, crossing and recrossing, each time a few yards higher up, until the whole has been thoroughly covered, takes time; but is far better that the angler's flies should be on the water, searching every spot fit to hold a fish. . . ."

On dry fly fishing, the authors write, "Dry-fly fishing, as practised in the South, differs slightly from the method here advocated for the rougher streams above-mentioned, inasmuch as the purist of the South will not throw a fly to any but a rising fish, even though he wait an hour or more before locating one, while the North Country angler not only throws to the rise, but also to such places as are likely to hold feeding fish."

It is interesting that in adapting dry fly fishing, north country anglers did not buy the whole idea of fishing the rise only. Similarly, when we started dry fly fishing here in America, we practiced it the way the north country anglers did and not according to the strict purist code of F. M. Halford.

Edmonds and Lee's greatest contribution to soft hackle fly literature is the matching of the fly pattern to the insect order each fly was supposed to represent. Pritt never attempted this. Skues could not say what certain soft-hackled flies imitated. And in my first book, I simply evaded the question because I, too, was without the knowledge.

The four orders represented and added earlier to the applicable patterns of Pritt are Ephemeridae (mayfly), Perlidae (stone fly), Trichoptera (caddis fly), and Diptera (common or true fly). Edmonds and Lee's list is included here. The descriptions of the patterns which they took from Pritt are not reprinted. Their own patterns are described verbatim.

1. Winter Brown — Perlidae
2. Waterhen Bloa — Ephemeridae
3. Greenwell's Glory. Hooks 1 or 2. — Ephemeridae

Wings: From a hen Blackbird's primary quill feather, bunched and split.
Body: Yellow silk, well waxed, ribbed with four turns of fine gold wire or tinsel.
Legs: Cochybondu Hen's hackle.
Head: Yellow silk, well waxed.

4. Spring Black (Pritt's Little Black) — Diptera
5. Dark Snipe or Snipe and Purple — Ephemeridae
6. Orange Partridge — Perlidae and Ephemeridae
7. Broughton's point or Dark Bloa — Ephemeridae
8. March Brown — Ephemeridae
9. Light Snipe or Snipe Bloa — Ephemeridae
10. Dark Needle (Pritt's dark Spanish) — Perlidae
11. Brown Owl — Trichoptera
12. Olive Bloa — Ephemeridae
13. Dark Watchet or Iron Blue Dun — Ephemeridae

14. Yellow Partridge   Perlidae and Diptera
15. Light Needle (Pritt's light Spanish)   Perlidae
16. Yellow-Legged Bloa   Ephemeridae
17. Dotterel   Ephemeridae
18. Poult Bloa   Ephemeridae
19. Gravel Bed (Pritt's Blue Partridge)   Diptera
20. Stone Midge   Diptera
21. Knotted Midge   Diptera
22. Black Gnat   Diptera
23. Ginger Spinner. Hooks 0 or 1.   Ephemeridae

Wings: Fibres of light grizzled blue Cock's hackle.
Body: Flat gold wire with a wrapping over it of orange silk, the silk to be untwisted and only one or two strands used.
Tail: Two strands from a ginger Cock's hackle.
Legs: Ginger Cock's hackle.
Head: Orange silk.

24. Dark Sedge. Hooks 1 or 2.   Trichoptera

Wings: Hackled with a reddish brown feather from the lesser coverts of a Tawny or Brown Owl's wing.
Body: Yellow silk, dubbed with brownish fawn Seal's fur.
Head: Brownish green herl from the tail of a cock Pheasant.

25a. Light Sedge. Hooks 1 or 2.   Trichoptera

Wings: Hackled with a light-barred reddish feather, from the lesser coverts of a Landrail's wing.
Body: Yellow silk, dubbed with reddish fur from the thigh of a Squirrel.
Head: A reddish herl from the tail of a cock Pheasant.

25b. Light Sedge. Hooks 1 or 2.   Trichoptera

Wings: From a light barred reddish feather, from the lesser coverts of a Landrail's wing (a larger feather than the one used for No. 25a), the outer side of the feather as the outside of the wing. Wings put on "penthouse" fashion.

Body: Same as No. 25a.

Legs: Reddish feather from the marginal coverts of a Landrail's wing.

Head: Same as No. 25a.

26. Red Spinner. Hook 1.   Ephemeridae

Wings: Fibres of medium grizzled blue Cock's hackle.

Body: Red silk, dubbed with maroon wool and ribbed with four turns of fine gold wire or tinsel.

Tail: Two strands from a deep red Cock's hackle.

Legs: Deep red Cock's hackle.

Head: Red silk.

27. July Dun   Ephemeridae
28. Rough-Bodied Poult   Ephemeridae
    (Pritt's Poult Bloa)
29. Pale Watery Dun   Ephemeridae
    (Pritt's July Dun)
30. Light Silverhorns. Hook 1.   Trichoptera

Wings: From a Thrush's secondary quill feather, the outer side of the feather as the outside of the wing, or from a Landrail's primary quill feather, the outer side of the feather as the outside of the wing. Wings put on "penthouse" fashion.

Body: Ash-coloured silk, sparingly dubbed with reddish grey fur from the thigh of a Squirrel.

Legs: Feather from a young Starling's thigh or flank.

Head: Ash-coloured silk.

Antennae: Two strands from a black and white feather from a Mallard's breast.

31. Dark Silverhorns. Hook 1.   Trichoptera

Wings: From a Waterhen's primary quill feather, the outer side of the feather as the outside of the wing. Wings put on "penthouse" fashion.

Body: Black silk, dubbed very sparingly with Mole's fur and

ribbed with olive silk.
Legs: Black Cock's hackle or green Plover's topping.
Head: Black silk.
Antennae: Two strands from a black and white feather from a Mallard's breast.

32.   August Dun. Hook 2.   Ephemeridae
Wings: From a Mallard's breast feather, lightly tinged with brown.
Body: Yellow silk, dubbed with yellow olive wool and ribbed with orange silk, sparingly spun with fur from the nape of a Rabbit's neck which has been lightly tinged red.
Tail: Two strands from a medium olive Cock's hackle.
Legs: Medium olive Hen's hackle.
Head: Yellow silk.

33.   Ant. Hook 0.   Hymenoptera
Wings: Hackled with a light blue Hen's hackle.
Body: Orange brown silk, dressed full at the tail with bronze Peacock herl, then a few turns of the silk towards the head, then dressed full at the shoulder with bronze Peacock herl.
Head: Orange brown silk.

34.   Green insect. Hooks 00 or 000.   Aphides
Wings: Hackled with a light blue Cock's hackle.
Body: Yellow silk, dubbed with bright green olive wool.
Head: Yellow silk.

Chapter V:

*Modern
Soft-Hackled Fly
Fishing Methods*

Droppers and Bobs

On water where the practice is permissible, using more than one soft hackle at a time can be very rewarding to the addict, particularly when he has not fished the water previously or is not familiar with its insect population. There are several obvious advantages. The first is that you can try more than one color or pattern of fly. The second is that you can try different sizes. And the third is that you can take two fish at the same time.

I was fishing an unpopular, large river in northwestern Wyoming during the fall of 1979. The river offered some of the finest riffles for soft-hackled fly fishing I have ever encountered. I wondered why the river didn't get more play than it did. Unbroken stretches seemed an eighth of a mile long with good fishing from head to tail. Whitefish far outnumbered brown and rainbow trout. But they took to the two-fly combination with relish. In a short time, I had four sets of Whitefish doubles, each fish averaging around 14 inches.

My general practice in fishing two flies at a time is to use a smaller one on the tail and a larger one on the "bob." I will also use opposite colors, or a light one on the tail and a dark one on the "bob."

One learns quickly about the selectivity of the trout and what might be going on in the river at the time, because it usually happens that only one of the patterns takes and the other does not, no matter where the taking fly is located. After you determine which is the taking fly, you can mount two of the takers on the tail and the "bob."

The two flies should be at least three feet apart. The "bob" fly is tied on one half of the blood knot which is left uncut after tying it. The length should be no longer than 12 inches, but this will shorten after you tie on succeeding soft hackles. I usually tie the "bob" fly on the heavier of the two leader sections because added stiffness helps hold the fly out at a nearly right angle to the leader itself, providing some additional action during the drift.

As has been said earlier, Pritt did not describe his fishing methods in "North-Country Flies." He did, however, outline his method for using three flies on a "cast" in "An Angler's Basket." It may be of some value to include that information here, too.

"On any ordinary rough stream during the spring it will be sufficient for any angler to confine himself in a general way to six flies, and with these chosen six he may fish day in and day out, anywhere and at any time, wet or fair, big water or little, sunshine or cloud, hot or cold."

Pritt made up two "casts" or leaders composed of three flies each, beginning with number one or the tail fly. "First cast.—1.

March-brown, hook No. 3, winged from a well-marked feather from the tail of a partridge, dubbed with a little hare's ear and yellow mohair mixed, the whole ribbed with a little yellow silk. This is an imitation of the natural male fly, the best feather being from a hen pheasant's quill; but the darker fly is usually, though not invariable, the better killer.

"2. Snipe and yellow (snipe bloa of the north).

"3. Woodcock, hackled with a well-marked feather from the outside of a woodcock's wing; body, orange silk, dubbed sparely with hare's ear.

"Second cast.—1. Water-hen bloa, hackled with a feather from the inside of a water-hen's wing (if you can find one with a blue tinge take that for preference); body, yellow silk, dubbed with fur from a water rat.

"2. Olive dun, winged from a starling's quill; body, greenish yellow silk, legs from a hen's neck, and stained to olive-yellow in onions.

"3. Dark snipe, hackled with a well-mottled feather from the outside of a snipe's wing; body, purple silk."

Long Distance Fishing

One of the best things about fishing the soft hackle is that you can do it from very long distances. And staying as far away from the fish as possible, as we all know, is one of the oldest angling mandates. You not only fish long, but you wade short. You start in at the head of a riffle and fish the longest line possible to cover the water at this position. The line is thrown straight across to the other side, then allowed to swing with the current until it is straight below you.

Let's say the riffle at this point is 60 feet wide. If you can cast an average of 60 feet, you can and should be casting into the head of the riffle from your bank or at least just a couple of feet from it. Now take a step downstream and cast the same length of line to the other side again. Follow the line down with your rod tip held low. Mend when you have to, but don't get into the habit of doing it without need.

As you move downstream through the riffle, try not to change the casting length of the line, but move in or out as the riffle widens or narrows. Try to cover all the water you can with each cast and keep casts close spaced. When you have fished to the tail of the riffle, you will have covered virtually all of the good, holding water and the slower and shallower water below you.

What I have tried to explain here is the "patterned casting" Paul Brown spoke about earlier. I don't agree with him that you have to "feel" the fly through the water, although you will begin to feel that you are steering the fly through the best part of the stream after you have caught some trout with the method.

Fishing soft hackles in this manner is different from other wet and dry fly methods. The deeply sunk nymph requires considerable line control, which, for most anglers means deep wading and relatively short casts. On many western streams, these anglers can be seen half way into the river, wading where they should be fishing. Similarly, traditional, upstream dry fly fishing requires deep wading and a shorter line because it must be pulled downstream ahead of the fly to keep it within striking distance and to prevent drag.

On Mending or Controlled Drag

Many experienced fly fishermen still don't practice mending as often as they should. Many of those that do, don't do it properly. The purpose of the mend is to take pressure off the fly and prevent its oblique racing across the current. The mend is usually made in the opposite direction of the belly of the line. It should be made without pulling the fly towards the angler. One way to do this is to carry excess line in large loops in your left hand. When the mend is made, line is fed from the hand loops, not ripped from the line and leader already on the water. This method also helps to lift the bellying portion of the line off the water. You will end up with more line on the water than when you started.

If you have excess line remaining when the fly has reached its furthest downstream point (before it starts to swing towards your bank), feed the remaining line into the guides and let the current pull it. This can add to the length of time the fly is "fishing" in the best part of the riffle or pool.

My interest in fishing the soft hackle slackens when the fly starts to swing across the current. And the closer it gets to my side of the river, the less effective and less efficient it becomes. In fact, it is in this part of the cast, where the largest number of false takes are experienced.

The reason for this is that the fish sees only the rear portion of the fly and generally misjudges it when he attacks. The most firmly hooked fish is the one which takes the soft hackle at the top of the cast, straight across from the angler. Here the fish sees the whole side of the fly, and intercepts it more easily and surely. The fly will often be hooked in the scissors portion of the jaw which is the best place to hook and hold any fish.

Normally, one doesn't have to set the hook in across-and-downstream soft hackle fly fishing. The fish charges at the fly and from his own greed or enthusiasm hooks himself. The pressure of the current against the line also helps. Whether I'm fishing off the reel or with the large loops in my left hand, the line is held loosely between my first finger and the cork handle. In this manner, I can let line be taken by the current or make my mend, by opening the finger. When a fish takes, I merely tighten my finger with the line under and against the cork grip, and raise the rod slightly. If the fish starts to run immediately, I use my finger as a brake until all of the excess line is pulled out and the fish is fighting off the reel.

When the fishing is good with soft hackles, I lose interest in fighting a fish for a long time, unless, of course, I feel it is a very large fish. Even then I hate to exhaust a fish just to get a better look at him. I also pinch the barbs down on all of my flies so the fish can be released more quickly and without damage. With no barb, it's not necessary to fight the fish to exhaustion to release it.

River Signs

A big "V" in the water is caused, of course, by a large, submerged or showing boulder, weed patch, or other obstacle. Wherever you find one of these in a pool or riffle, it will be the most obvious place to take a trout on the soft hackle. In fact, the water may fish poorly above and below it, but where the "V" is, the fish are. One should approach the "V" cautiously and move towards it along the fisherman's bank. It is folly to try to fish both sides of the "V" at the same time. Rather, the angler should concentrate on the side of the "V" closest to him, first. This will be quite ordinary fishing. The fly should be pitched several feet ahead of the point of the "V" and allowed to swing down along the closest side. Try this a few times to make sure you have covered it well.

If the fisherhman's bank is a well trod one, the fish will lie normally on the far side of the "V." But it pays to work both sides anyway. Fishing the far side is a little more complicated, because of the complex currents created by the obstacle. What you have basically are two fast pieces of water separated by almost dead still water or even water which is going in opposite direction.

Keeping the line up and over the conflicting currents is the best plan. You may have to wade closer to the "V" to do this and a long rod will help. Once you get within short casting distance, throw the fly high above the point of the "V" and raise the line high enough so that it is free of the currents. Only a short part of the line and all of the leader will be in the water, but the fly will be drifting quite naturally where, in most cases, the fish will be. If nothing happens on the first or second cast, move down one step and try again, and repeat the process until you are well below the effects of the "V."

There is another kind of "V" formed when two separate pieces of streamy water come together. It might be called "inverted" because the legs of it face upstream, not downstream as the one just described. The inverted "V" is not formed by a visible obstacle so it is more difficult to see. In my experience, this can be the hottest part of a riffle, particularly for migrating fish. They have a choice to make before going upstream and I think they hold there, at or below the point, trying to decide which side they're going to take. When you find an inverted "V," slow down. Make short casts to the closest arm, then lengthen the cast to cover the other arm. After you've fished both sides, move down into the unified stream and fish it carefully.

High Rods

There are two other situations which can be served by the same method used for the downstream "V." The first is when you have a fast, narrow stream of water in an otherwise large river. And again, if the fisherman's bank is a well trod one, chances are the fish will be on the opposite side of the stream.

You can almost ignore your side and concentrate on the far side by wading as close to the stream as you can, then casting and holding the rod very high for the line to clear the water.

The second is over a weedbed. A weedbed between you and the water you want to fish will slow that part of the line over it. The higher the weeds, the slower the water, and, of course, the more severe the drag. In this kind of situation, the angler could cast over the bed into the flowing water, and make frequent mends downstream to keep up with the faster moving line end and leader. The better way is to get as close to the bed as possible, cast into the flowing water and hold the rod high for the line to clear the bed.

There is such a spot on one of my favorite rivers. The flowing water runs between the weed bed and a long submerged rock ledge on the other side. If the pool has not been disturbed for an hour or more before I get into it, one, two, or three trout will be taken as I proceed through it.

The fishing here is challenging. When I first started fishing the pool some years ago, I lost fish after fish in the weed bed. Then, not too long ago, I learned something about this kind of water which I think will work wherever you have a similar situation. As soon as you hook a fish, turn around facing upstream, hold the rod high and bending backward and march right upstream and towards your bank as fast as you can. The fish will follow in most cases. Once he is clear of the weed bed, you can turn around and fight him in the weed-free water.

One thousand one. . .one thousand two. . .one thousand. . .

After many years of fly fishing, I have begun to talk to myself while fishing a riffle. Not talking exactly but counting. I start my personal conversation as soon as the fly hits the water. "One thousand one, one thousand two, one thousand three," and so on. I guess I want to know how long it takes for the fly to fish the water. Or possibly how long before a fish attacks the fly.

In rivers of known, total water speed, it is interesting that one riffle will fish a lot faster than the one above it or below it. On one western river, for example, a 60-foot line will fish through three different riffles at different speeds. The top one is the slowest at about 18 seconds, the middle one at about 14 seconds and the last one at about 11 seconds. During the last couple of years, the 11 second riffle for me has been the most productive.

Each of the three riffles fish faster at the top and slow down towards the tail. This is only natural. But there is a lesson in it. Make more frequent casts in the top part of the riffle than in the lower part.

All this leads, of course, to what might be the slowest water in which one might fish soft hackles in the traditional manner of straight across to straight below. Based on my counting, and with the 60-foot line, I would say that any riffle that doesn't fish in under 25 seconds might be too slow for the soft hackle to be effective. More fishing time can be added to any riffle by throwing the fly higher in the stream.

Upstream Techniques

Nothing is more frustrating to the addict than trying to fish soft hackles in the across and downstream method on slow, glassy, oily water. Rivers like the Letort, Henry's Fork, Silver Creek and other similar waters were not made for downstream soft hackles. The floating line will snake pitifully in these waters, the fly following the snake on the surface and leaving a wake. A fast sinking line might work in this kind of water, because the complex surface effects would not be as pronounced on a line, all of which could be several inches below the surface.

The best way to fish soft hackles in this kind of water is to turn upstream and fish them exactly like a dry fly. Edmonds and Lee's system, outlined earlier, might be a suitable method. Well-known, dry fly aficionados have told me they are now using soft hackles in this manner with excellent results. Some of them oil the fly and false cast to throw off extraneous moisture. They use the thorax patterns which can imitate nymphs and emergers. The fly, however, does not sit up on the surface like a dry fly and requires keen eyesight and attention. Strike slowly to the rise.

Fishing Both Sides—With Reservations

A nice, broken, fast-flowing riffle can be deceptive to the soft-hackled fly addict. It all looks good and if the angler can cast far enough and often enough, he will probably cover the productive water as well as the unproductive. There are hotspots, however, which are worth paying more attention to when you encounter them. One of these will be a deep hole on the side of the main stream of the river, which can change from year to year depending on springtime floods. It is possible to miss such water when it is located on the unpopular side of the river. So it is a good idea to fish both sides of the river if possible. I made this mistake last fall on one of my favorite pieces of water. I approached it from the angler's side as I always did and experienced very poor sport. Around the third day, I decided to cross the river, walk way up and fish it down. Not much happened until I was about two thirds through the water. The strike came quite close to my bank. I landed the fish and released it. I continued and took another fish a few feet from the first one. Several more steps downstream and I was approaching the water where the fish hit. With each step, the water got deeper and deeper. I was perplexed because the deep water was never here before. The water nearly came to the top of my waders.

Now I looked across the stream to see where I would be in relation to the hole, fishing from the other side. The next time through from the regular bank, I paused longer at the spot than usual. It required a long cast to reach it, but on the first cast, I took a nice brown in practically the same water I fished from the other side. For the rest of two weeks fishing in the area, the deep water was the most productive in the whole riffle, no matter which side you fished it from, and no matter who fished it.

Normally, when more than two anglers are fishing the bigger western rivers, they all fish it from the same side, that is, wading in the shallow waters and casting to the deep. And as long as there are anglers lined up in the riffle, this is the way it should be, for anyone fishing the deep side would ruin the fishing for the others. Understandably, young, strong anglers or strangers to your river will do this. Invariably, they start to catch fish where the three or four anglers fishing from the other side are catching none. The reason for this is that all of a sudden the fish are seeing a fly swinging in the opposite direction from what they've been seeing all day.

If a riffle or pool is unoccupied by other anglers, it might be worth the trip over to the other side to give the trout a completely different look at the fly. However, as soon as anglers appear on the regular side of the river, you should get out and join the line on the other side or move away from the riffle.

This is good streamside etiquette, but there is much more to it. There is relatively little outstanding water to be shared by a large number of anglers, particularly during certain times of the year. Rules of etiquette are not written in state and national park angling regulations, although they should be. They do give limits and dates and methods to be legally employed. That's the letter of the law. A few anglers subscribe to it by getting into a popular riffle and occupying the hot spot. They have come a thousand miles or more and will spend nearly that many dollars or more to enjoy a week's fishing on some great water. But many other anglers have done the same thing. If they all fished in the manner they thought was their due and still according to regulations, fishing would be almost impossible for many and available for only those few.

To permit everyone to have a go on the best riffles of many major western streams and even those in the midwest, it is suggested that you fish as many of my friends do on these popular waters: with some reservation and courtesy.

Rule No. 12 of the Strathspey Angling Improvement Association at Grantown on Spey, Scotland, says it very nicely: "No angler shall cut in front of another when fishing a pool, but each angler shall take his turn of fishing in order of his arrival at the pool, and must move at least one yard after every cast."

The "one yard after every cast," sounds a bit harsh. On the rivers I fish, a step is enough, and I don't think my friends would start screaming if one took even two casts before stepping downstream for the next. It is sad, too, to watch an angler obey the law and kill his limit according to it. It is egoistic to believe that the free trout dinner will help pay for the trip. In my annual three weeks to my favorite fishing place every autumn, I see hundreds of good sized trout caught and all of them released. If my friends and I go out for dinner, invariably someone orders trout, even though the ones he released would have tasted much better.

Fishing Winds

The inexperienced angler will curse all winds because he doesn't know how to handle them. Actually some winds can be advantageous to the angler. For average right-handed casters, the upstream wind facilitates false casting and helps to lengthen the cast with tighter loops and fewer wind knots. The same wind also helps the angler to make the more prevalent upstream mends, but will hinder the performance of the downstream ones.

Downstream winds of high velocity are the worst for the right-handed caster when he's fishing from the downtream, left side of the stream. It blows the line below intended trajectory. The line hits the rod on the back cast. The fly and the leader are frequently caught between the line and the rod in the region of the top guides.

In severe downstream winds, I cast across my left shoulder, keeping the line trajectory below me. I lose casting distance this way but I can go on fishing. Another method is to cast over your right shoulder with your hand cocked or bent over at the wrist and pointing downstream. This forces the line to move in a trajectory below the rod. It is a very difficult fly casting maneuver. The timing and the degree of cocking are critical, both having to be changed as the speed of the wind changes. I can't do this cast myself, but my friend, Paul Brown, now one of the most severely addicted western locals, does it beautifully.

One can also turn the downstream wind into an advantage by crossing the river and fishing it from the right downstream side. The other alternative is to find stretches of the river which turn sufficiently to be unaffected by wind direction.

The Ancient Mystery

Why is it one can take fish after fish on soft hackles in a riffle one day and fail to experience even the slightest pull of a fish on the same flies in the same riffle the next? All conditions seem to be the same. And the time is the same.

When this happens to me, and it will happen to you, I leave the normally productive part of the riffle and seek out the trout in the rougher and shallower parts of the immediate water. I will go upstream making quick short casts. And I will try the far bank. Fish normally found in the deeper part of a riffle, will, for some reason and at certain times, line up along the nearest, far bank, (the untrod one,) even though the water there will only be a few inches deep. To cast to these fish, you might have to wade right through the middle of the normally productive riffle, but you already know nothing is taking there anyway.

Drop the fly as close to the bank as possible with repeated short casts and short drifts. The fly will quickly start to swing towards you in the deeper part of the riffle away from the fish. In most cases, you will find the fish there. If you don't, it's time to get out, sit on the bank and think about the inevitable uncertainties of trout fishing.

One last, little fishing tip will help you look good to other fishermen on a crowded stream, yet save valuable time when you have to retrieve all of your line to change or inspect the fly and leader. It was taught to me by a professional guide and goes as follows: with the floating line trailing in the current straight below you, lower the rod tip to keep it parallel to the river surface. Bring the rod up smartly, lifting the line and leader off the water as though you were going to make a backcast. Check the rod at the top of the cast and the line and leader will come flying at you. Concentrate on the middle or butt section of the leader and catch it in your left hand as it passes low over your left side. Deftness is all and beware of the hook.

Chapter VI

*Soft-Hackled
Flies Revisited
and Refined*

We soft-hackled fly addicts are very lucky, indeed, to have available all of the hackles and other materials we need to make all of the patterns of today, and many of the older patterns listed in Pritt and Edmonds and Lee. It's true that a few feathers they called for are no longer available to us, but their colors can be easily matched by others and through dyeing by looking at the plates. This is one reason why they were included.

Until 1977, and for quite a few years before that, the importation of the plumage of many wild birds was prohibited into the United States.

In 1978, however, new regulations were passed by the Convention of International Trade in Endangered Species of Wildlife. It agreed that since gamebirds are used for human consumption and that none of these birds are on the endangered list, the feathers from them could be freely exported to the U.S. Many non-game birds are also killed in England and other countries as vermin, and their plumage is also included in the list. E. Veniard Ltd, England's largest and most reliable fly tying material house, for example, can now send us the feathers from coot, French partridge, golden plover, grouse, jackdaw, ostrich, partridge, snipe, woodcock, magpie and starling. Many American distributors have also begun to stock many of these feathers.

Genuine silk tying threads and flosses are also still available from Veniard's. They offer 20 colors of Pearsall's Gossamer tying silks and 14 colors of Marabou silk floss. You should order these materials in matching colors so that you can use the same tying thread as the body floss. The Marabou comes double stranded which must be split into two strands before winding. Other tying threads and flosses can be used providing you can get them in the proper colors.

Other good sources for game bird hackles are the shooting preserves which have sprung up around the country. Most of these shoot pheasants, chukars, and partridges. The birds are skinned by the preserve operators, who will sell entire skins at very reasonable prices. One preserve near Chicago will sell complete partridge skins for $4.00 each. Many fly fishermen also shoot game birds. If you don't happen to be one of these, you should make friends with those who do to guarantee your own supply of these hackles.

Another way to obtain rare colors not available from any bird is to dye natural gray partridge hackles. I choose partridge because they are the lightest colored feathers and take dyes more truly than darker colored feathers. The color plates in this book show several different colors available with Veniard dyes, as well as natural body and wing hackles.

The process is very simple. Heat a small amount of water,

(about two cups) to near boiling. Pour in a half teaspoon of the dye and stir. Place a handful of hackles in the liquid and let them simmer for a few minutes. Examine a few hackles by holding them up to a light. Wet, they will appear darker than when they are dried. Let the hackles stew until you have the desired shade. Then pour the liquid and the hackles into a kitchen strainer. Run cold water over the hackles and dump them on several thicknesses of newspapers. Separate the hackles and spread them out on the newspapers. The hackles will look very messy and useless, but in a few minutes they will dry, open up and assume their natural, original shape.

Other sources for feathers for soft-hackled flies (and neglected by the author until only recently) are natural hen-feathers. Several of these are also illustrated in the color plates. The necks are very inexpensive. Feathers are small and more spade-shaped than the long, thin, triangular cock hackles. Colors range from off whites to duns to brown and reds. Multi-color furnace, badger, and plymouth rocks are also available. Hen necks look "dirty" and many of the feathers are imperfectly marked, a desirable feature for soft hackles.

Choosing the right size of feather for the size of the hook has been a problem for many addicts I have met or heard from through correspondence. I have devised a chart which should make it very easy to pick the correct size of hackle for a given size hook. The chart pertains to partridge and grouse only because feathers from starling, snipe, jackdaw and other birds do not vary much in size, and do not give you as large a selection to choose from. At any rate, you simply lay a feather over the outline of the size fly you're tying to get the approximate right size. The size of the feather is not critical, except in the extreme smaller sizes. In fact, you may choose feathers with longer barbs (those which might extend beyond the normal position of the beginning of the bend) to obtain more hackle motion.

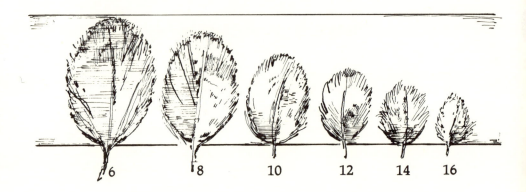

The smallest soft hackles I ever made were size 20's. Feathers for this small a fly are hard to find and difficult to hold on to after you apply sufficient plier pressure to wrap them. If you want soft hackles in this size, I suggest you use a larger hook, say a 14 or 16, with a body only half the length of the hook and with the smallest partridge, grouse or other feather you can find. On these small patterns, it is also advisable to tie the hackle on the hook with its tip instead of its stem. Barbules at the end are much shorter than at the stem and often will be more vividly colored than the others.

The largest soft hackles I ever made were on 4 and 6 low water hooks for a friend of mine who is an avid and frequent steelhead fisherman, and who, in 1979, was fortunate enough to fish the last four days of the salmon season on the Matapedia. One of the oversize flies I suggested he try for the salmon was the heron tups. This is tied exactly like the small tups, but with a heron hackle at the head. The barbs on these hackles are up to two inches long. Two wraps of this feather makes an artificial unlike anything you, or any fish, have ever seen. During the end of his four days on the river, my friend decided to try the outlandish tups. He took two grilse immediately, the limit on the river. The entry in the fishing log at the end of that day read, "two grilse on soft hackles." It is probably the only salmon fishing log book in the world to include such an entry. My friend also used the same fly the following autumn on his favorite western steelhead river and reported taking a 10 pound steelhead on it.

Now, I have heard from other sources that soft hackles are being used for steelhead. My recommendation for these patterns is to tie them on low water hooks, with the bodies covering less than half of the hook. The patterns can be "dressed up" with either gold or silver ribs.

Frequently I have been asked which soft-hackled fly is the most effective. This is a difficult question to answer. Knowing something about the river helps. For example, I will fish the thorax patterns in water known for high populations of caddis flies. I will use the unthoraxed flies in a mayfly spinner fall because they are more delicate and imitate more closely the fully matured insects. In fast, rough water, I like the thorax patterns because there's more to them, hence, they are more easily seen. If you're on water earlier than an expected hatch, you should definitely fish the thoraxed patterns, preferably in the colors corresponding to the hatching insects.

The question of size comes up frequently, too. Twelves and fourteens are the most popular for resident fish. Tens and eights are used more frequently for migrating browns and rainbows. The hook, itself, should be a sproat. Veniard's still sells the best of this kind of hook, which is made for them by Partridge.

Since the publication of "The Soft-Hackled Fly," I have added several patterns to the original list, which, I and other addicts have used with considerable success on many rivers. Old and new patterns are fully illustrated in the color section, as well as on the dust jacket. First here are the original dressings. Hook sizes are 10 to 16.

1. **Partridge and orange**
Body: Orange silk floss
Hackle: Brown partridge

2. **Partridge and green**
Body: Green silk floss
Hackle: Gray partridge

3. **Partridge and yellow**
Body: Yellow silk floss
Hackle: Brown or gray partridge

4. **Partridge and orange and fur thorax**
Body: 2/3's orange silk floss
Thorax: Black and brown hare's face
Hackle: Brown partridge

5. **Partridge and green and fur thorax**
Body: 2/3's green silk floss
Thorax: Black and brown hare's face
Hackle: Gray partridge

6. **Partridge and yellow and fur thorax**
Body: 2/3's yellow silk floss
Thorax: Light brown hare's face

Hackle: Brown or gray partridge

7. **Tup's Indispensable**
Body: 2/3's yellow silk floss
Thorax: Light pink and orange fur, (correctly colored fur available from Veniard)
Hackle: Light partridge dyed in Veniard Iron Blue Dun

8. **Iron Blue Dun**
Tail: Four or five whisks of white hen barbs
Tag: Red tying silk (same color as the tying thread)
Body: Mole's fur spun very thinly on the red tying silk
Hackle: Short jackdaw or starling

9. **Snipe and purple**
Body: Purple silk floss
Hackle: Small covert hackle from snipe wing or starling

10. **Pheasant Tail**
Body: Two or three or more herls of the center tail of a rooster pheasant wound on together with very thin copper wire. Wire can be twisted with the herls and tied on together, or wound on separately after herls are in place.
Hackle: Brown or gray partridge

The pheasant tail, in one form or another, is probably the most popular of all soft hackles. Its medium, rusty brown color can imitate a large number of caddis and mayfly insects in nymph, pupal, and adult stages. Not too long ago, I had the opportunity to purchase some high quality golden rooster pheasant tail feathers. I substituted barbs from these feathers for those of the common pheasant with a slight difference. The body was lighter and marked differently. From this, it occurred to me that barbs from other large birds such as goose, heron, turkey, duck, etc., could also be used as bodies for effective soft hackles.

The reason for the fuzzy, "buggy" look of these herls is the opening up of the beard or scroll-like plates which line every barbule as the stem is wound around the hook. In the birds' flight these plates or hooks interact with their partners on adjacent barbs, opening when flight power is not needed and closing to create a tighter vane when it is needed.

11. Snipe and yellow
Body: Yellow silk floss
Hackle: Small covert or underwing hackle from snipe wing or starling

12. March brown spider
Body: Mixed hair from hare's face
Rib: Narrow gold
Hackle: Brown partridge
Tying silk: Orange

13. Grouse and orange
Body: Orange silk floss
Hackle: Black and orange grouse hackle or woodcock

14. Starling and herl
Body: Peacock herl
Hackle: Small covert hackle from starling wing or body

New patterns:

15. Pheasant tail with fur thorax

Body: 2/3's rooster tail and copper wire
Thorax: Very dark hare's face
Hackle: Dark partridge

16. Golden pheasant tail with fur thorax
Body: 2/3's golden pheasant tail and copper wire
Thorax: Light hare's face
Hackle: Medium partridge

17. Cumberland
Body: Red or orange silk floss
Hackle: Medium partridge
Rib: Narrow gold wire

John Waller Hills believed this fly to be the most effective sunk fly on the Test, particularly on hot days and in slow water.

18. Dean's black
Body: Rear 2/3's peacock herl wrapped thickly; front 1/3 black wool or dubbed fur
Hackle: Iron blue dun dyed partridge
Rib: Silver heavy wire

Dean Yannias, editor of this book, tied this fly for big, western rivers. It is probably taken for the prevalent stoneflies, in the larger sizes.

19. Black and red dun
Body: Rear 2/3's red wool or dubbed fur; front 1/3 black wool or dubbed fur
Hackle: Iron blue dun dyed partridge
Rib: Narrow silver wire

Another imitation of a variety of stone fly nymphs.

20. Brown Drake
Body: Dark brown or chocolate floss
Thorax: Darkest hare's face
Hackle: Dyed dark brown partridge

This fly was developed for fishing the Pere Marquette during the brown drake hatch which normally comes off before and after Memorial day weekend. The insects rarely appear before dusk, but when they do, they come in large masses, during which times the trout feed ravenously on them. It is usually too dark to fish dry, but this artificial thrown three or four feet ahead of the noisy rises produces satisfying results. It is another example of the high efficiency of a soft hackle fished slightly upstream to rising trout when conditions make it difficult to fish dry. The thorax should be kept very thin.

Admittedly, the soft-hackled fly is one of the easiest of all artificials to tie. The basic patterns are made of just two parts, the body and the hackle. A little fur is added to the thorax patterns. Any experienced tier should be able to make a dozen an hour of the same pattern, if he has materials and hooks laid out in front of him.

You begin by tying the thread towards the head of the fly. Tie in the floss. In handling the floss, keep your hands clean and your fingers smooth. Wind the floss toward the rear of the hook in very wide and flat turns, then come back to where you started. (Figure A) Try not to add appreciably to the diameter of the hook. This gives you a smooth body with no humps. You can wind with your fingers, in which case you should grab the floss at the same position every revolution. You can also wind the floss by attaching a pair of hackle pliers to the floss, in which case you never touch it.

Now choose the hackle using the guide for the right size.

Strip the soft fuzz off the bottom portion of the hackle. (Figure B) Pull several of the barbs on each side of the feather downwards toward the stem. (Figure C) Tie the stem on the hook, with the natural bend of the feather pointing towards the tail.

The number of wraps depends on the hackle. If it is thick and full, once around is enough. Thinner feathers will require one and a half turns, but rarely two. How does the tier use one and a half turns and still tie off under the hook? One way is to tie the hackle stem onto the hook below the beginning of the barbs. With this method, the tier actually wraps the first turn or a good part of it without barbs on the stem. The position of the stem at the contact point on the hook shank can be raised or lowered to give a thinner or thicker look to the fly. (Figure D)

The direction of tying the hackle is another point of discussion. It is natural to wrap hackles of any kind over the top of the hook and away from the tier, that is, in the same natural direction of the tying thread. For some time, I have been doing the opposite. I wind the hackle backwards, under the hook shank, because I feel that the hackle is more firmly tied down when the hackle and the thread meet each other from opposite directions.

The thread will be behind the wound hackle when you have finished this far. Now you must bring the thread up through the hackle to finish off. Do this slowly and carefully, winding the thread through the barbs to make sure you don't tie them down. (Figure E)

We'll stop here for a moment and explain how to spin the thorax and where to put it if you were tying a thorax pattern. With thorax patterns, less than two thirds of the hook is covered with floss. The fur, be it hare's face, seal's fur, mole or possum is cut up or pulled apart into 1/8 inch pieces. Wax the portion of the tying thread to receive the fur. Pick up small sections of the fur and place them against the thread. (Figure F) You'll need less than you think. You can spin the fur two ways. The easiest is to pinch the fur and the tying thread and roll them back and forth between your thumb and forefinger until a loose noodle is formed. The other is to cut the thread from the bobbin, letting it hang loose and spinning it in one direction. The second method produces a looser thorax with more hairs sticking out perpendicularly to the thread.

Now, wind the threaded fur onto the hook to form the thorax and proceed with the hackle as described before.

It is a simple matter to tie herl heads on soft hackles as prescribed by Pritt. After you have wound the thread through the hackle, tie in the thinner end of the herl. Carry the tying thread to the eye, then bring up the herl in even wraps and finish off with a whip finish.

Adapting your own soft hackles for nymphing, bulging, and rising trout still does not require entomological knowledge. It doesn't require, in a book like this, charts which match artificial fly to living insect; emergence dates; and Latin or Greek names, the pronunciation of which leave many anglers speechless. It only requires matching of color and size to imitate many of the mayflies and caddis flies you might encounter on your favorite river.

Carl Richards feels this is true. "The soft hackle is the best imitation of emerging caddis, from a size 6 orange to a 22 black. The fly, in the right color and size, also imitates hundreds of emerging mayflies. Take the green drake hatch on the Henry's Fork, for example. This is tough fishing. You never feel you have the right fly. You might catch 20 fish a

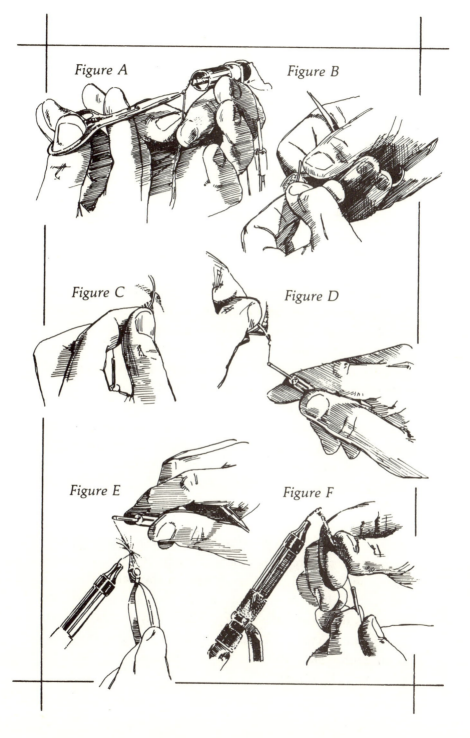

day, but you feel you ought to take 100. I tied a soft hackle which worked better than the dry flies we were using. The hackle is a gray partridge, dyed greenish yellow. And the body is light green fur, ribbed with yellow silk. You can call such a fly a floating hackle or even a dry fly soft hackle.

"The soft hackle is also a better imitation of the mayfly during the stage when its wings are unfolding. The natural fly struggles in this stage for a long time before its wings are perfectly formed.

"It's up to the angler to choose the colors which represent the insects he's trying to imitate. Silk bodies are fine for caddis. Thorax, or all fur bodies are better for mayflies."

Carl suggested we use the super hatches section from his and Doug Swisher's book, "Selective Trout," as a guide to tying soft hackles which might do as well as their own list. There are 14 patterns. All but one asks for gray wings in one shade or another, so the dominant hackle should be gray partridge. All the patterns are tied with fur bodies in brown, tan, olive, cream, and blue/black (mole.) Omit tails. Keeping the same colored hackle, it's possible, then, to tie only five soft hackles which might cover the 14 in the super hatches section.

Carl's endorsement of the soft-hackled fly is much appreciated.

"Selective Trout," is among the world's best selling books on angling, due, perhaps to its original concepts and incredible depth of research and study of the insects trout feed on. When I visited Carl's place in Michigan soon after the book was published, I was amazed to see mayflies and caddis flying about his office and laboratory. The newly hatched insects came from several aquariums used for the earlier study and photography. He pointed to one of them and said, "that's the Ephemerella flavilinea."

Chapter VII:

Upper Big Blue

A Short Story

Author's note
This is the kind of short story that no angling publication would care to publish. Angling magazines rarely publish fiction except that amount of it which writers accidentally weave into their material. General fiction magazines would not be interested in it because the subject is fly fishing. Because of these reasons, it appears here.

They came down the river fishing slowly and intently, the three unpaddled canoes barely moving in the black, slow water. Jack was downstream leading his clients. He had a trout on, landed it and threw it unceremoniously into the canoe with the others. He was doing what he had told his clients to do earlier, when they had started. That was to keep the trout for a cookout in the screened gazebo at Perkins Landing. Would they like that...a real upper Big Blue cookout with fried trout and bacon, hamburgers, potatoes, baked beans and salad?

They couldn't say no.

So it was arranged. Jack's young wife, Sadie, would drive to the landing on the old log road and bring with her the groceries and the whiskey, gin, beer and wine. She could start the fires on the outdoor grills and chill the beverages in Perkins Creek.

Now, as Jack neared the landing, he began to wonder if she had made it in with their old, dilapidated pickup. He looked downstream and saw smoke coming up through the pines. She made it, he said to himself. Good old girl.

At the landing, Jack ground the canoe up the sandy bank, wedging it between two large boulders. He scooped the small trout out of the canoe and removed the dragging landing net. There was one can of beer left in the net. Jack had drunk the rest of the six pack during the three hour trip down the river. He started up to the gazebo and noticed that Sadie was not alone. It was his friend, Wendell, drink in hand.

"Howdy, Wendell, when did you get in?"

Wendell raised his glass. "I've been up north. Thought I'd stop and see you on the way home. Sadie invited me to the cookout. Hope your clients won't mind. I followed her in my new Grand Prix."

"They're nice people. Good, sporting fly fishermen. They'd be glad to meet you. I've got to clean the trout."

Jack walked over to the creek, dropped the remaining beer in it and cleaned the trout. Before he returned to the gazebo, he poured bourbon into a tin cup, held it under a miniature waterfall in the creek and returned. Inside the gazebo, he resumed his salutations with Wendell.

Wendell was 20 years older than Jack. Their relationship

had started as client and guide a few years before, but now they were just friends. Wendell was working on a book on fly fishing and carried his pencilled manuscript with him whenever he knew he would be around fishing people. Between sips of his drink, he pretended to read his work. He looked up at Jack.

"I found the kind of illustrations I need for the book."

Wendell had cut several color plates out of one of the more successful books on fly fishing and had pasted them on sheets which were inserted into the manuscript. He showed them to Jack.

Jack recognized them immediately. "From Schweibert's 'Matching the Hatch.' Real nice. Hope you can do as well."

"I'm thinking of macro-photography of the real insects. All I have to do now is collect them."

Angling books and fishing talk bored Jack. He, himself, was a fine artist and had studied in Chicago. He could appreciate such work as Schwiebert's, but he also had met other, experienced anglers who were "writing a book," and he was a bit tired of it all. He found this an excuse to refill his tin cup and got up to leave.

"Can I fill you up again, Wendell?"

"I hate to impose, but I want to pay for my share . . . for the booze and all."

"You know how we are, Wendell. We never worry about things like that."

Jack was out of the gazebo, headed for the creek when he saw one of the canoes pulling up to the landing. He set the tin cups down and walked down to help them in.

It was the young couple. Jack guided the prow of the canoe up the sandy bank and helped the girl out. She was an attractive, athletic type. She needed very little help, but reached out to Jack's hand.

Jack asked if she had enjoyed the ride and she replied, "It was super. We saw a deer and her fawn drinking on the bank. And we caught some fish and kept them for the cookout, didn't we Charles?"

Charles nodded his head. "It was nice. Like you said, Jack, there are a lot of trout in the upper Big Blue. The flies you gave us worked well on them. Here's Phil and Carol. I think they did well, too."

The last canoe pulled up. Phil and Carol were an older couple. Coming into the landing between the other canoes, Phil banged into one of them, showing his inexperience. Jack ran over to help and got them both out without either getting their feet wet. Jack saw the trout in the bottom of the canoe. "I knew you could take them, Phil. How was the canoe ride?"

"You know how I feel about canoes. But it was an easy, enjoyable ride and I was able to fish water that I could never get to any other way. Carol enjoyed it, too."

By now, Sadie and Wendell had come down to greet the two parties. A new drink in his hand, Wendell was introduced to the couples. Jack said, "Wendell is joining us for the cookout. He's an old friend and a good fly fisherman. Let's all go up to Perkins and have a drink."

II.

Perkins Landing was named for the long dead log baron, Ken Perkins. He built the landing and the log road from it in the 1890s, when logging flourished in the area. From his estate was also built the screened gazebo, free to use by modern day canoeists and campers.

The landing divided the upper Big Blue into two different

and distinct kinds of water. Above, where Jack and his clients were fishing, the river was winding, slow and sluggish and black from the rotten vegetation of the surrounding swamps. Here, were the indigenous, dark, red-bellied brook trout, eager and dumb. And fat and wily brown trout, hardy ancestors of the first brown trout planted in the stream by the same log baron at the turn of the century. The upper Big Blue was best fished from canoes.

Below the landing, the river cleared itself over long straight stretches of gravel. Solid banks replaced the soggy ones above. And where the river took on speed and where it narrowed, it shot itself through in white-plumed chutes, delighting experienced canoeists and terrorizing beginners.

One such chute lay just downstream of the landing, and, when the wind died down in the trees, the roaring of the chute could be heard in the gazebo.

III.

When they talked in the gazebo, it was obvious that Wendell and Phil could not see eye to eye about anything. This was especially true about trout fishing. Wendell was a dry fly man; Phil primarily a wet fly fisherman. Wendell liked fishing from a canoe and could be called expert in his handling of the craft in any kind of water. Phil's experience ranked him as a novice, and because of this, he actually feared to be on white water in the frail craft.

He made this trip with Charles and his wife only because he thought it would be a nice outing for the wives. Besides, Charles, before he was married, canoed extensively in many parts of the country.

Phil was skeptical about canoeing the upper Big Blue, but Jack assured him anybody could make the trip down to Perkins. And he was right. Phil actually enjoyed it. The water was slow. The fishing was good. And his wife enjoyed what he normally shared alone. Phil was first to sense his and Wendell's disagreements so when he heard about the book, he decided to ask Wendell about it.

Wendell beamed. "Trout are far more selective in their feeding habits than most fly fisherman realize. This is especially true in dry fly fishing where the fish has the opportunity to see the same natural fly over and over again. When the angler puts a fly over him, it better be the exact copy, color-for-color, size-for-size and shape-for-shape, or the trout will have nothing to do with it. Many of the old classic flies just do not resemble the naturals the way they're supposed to. And when anglers use them, they can't understand why they can't take rising trout. They're just too smart."

Phil smiled at the last remark. He was thinking of the line from an older writer who said he thought a trout had the brain of a lizard.

Wendell went on. "I've developed a series of dry flies which are really effective on selective trout. They're different from anything anyone has ever come up with. That's what the book's about."

Phil listened carefully. His approach to fly fishing was passionate, not scientific. His trout fishing was fun, not study. His old wet fly patterns were good enough for him now, as they had been for many years. He could not believe the simple trout was as educated as Wendell made him out to be. He wanted to ask Wendell about wet fly fishing, but he knew if he did, it would widen their discussion further and add to their obvious differences.

So he took up conversation with Sadie who was busy with the cooking. He had met her during the previous fishing season when he stopped at her husband's tackle shop. The shop was a room on the side of an old run-down farm house on the river road. The house was without water or electricity. There was no central heating, just a wood stove in the kitchen adjoining the shop. The house was in a state of slow rehabilitation, and even though Jack was a big, strong, young man and talented with saw and hammer, his work on the house came slowly and only when he felt like it or was "inspired."

The only part of the house that had a finished look was the shop. Jack's artistic talent showed through here. He equipped it with fine, old glass-enclosed cabinets. Angling artifacts hung about the room. Framed angling prints hung from the walls, as did fine, black-and-white sketches created by Jack, himself. There was a wood stove in the shop, too, with an enameled coffee pot on it at all times. Coffee was free as was information about the fishing.

When Phil entered the shop and met Sadie and Jack, he thought they felt they never cared if they sold anything at all. He also thought the inventory of Hardy reels, expensive lines, and bamboo rods seemed of a quality and quantity far more necessary than was needed for a shop of such meager potential. But Phil loved it immediately, and he couldn't help but admire Jack and Sadie for their hardiness and their apparent genuineness. They were to him pioneer types, escapees from business and careers, family and responsibility.

In the gazebo, he talked animatedly with Sadie, while the smells of the various foods heightened all conversation and whetted the thirsts of the other persons in it.

IV.

They had eaten well and drunk much. Jack and Wendell were really quite drunk, tottering when standing, and sprawling when sitting. Conversation started to move toward the canoe ride down the river. Jack said, weaving, "I'll go first. Charles and his wife can come behind me. And Phil and Carol can follow them. Sarah and Wendell can haul the groceries and stuff up to the pickup and Wendell's car. We'll meet them at the house."

This bit of news of a nighttime canoe ride down the rest of the river came as quite a shock to Phil. He was under the notion from the beginning that the canoe ride was to Perkins Landing only and he quickly reminded Jack of this. "I could never make it down the river in the dark. I don't think I would try it in broad daylight."

Jack couldn't hear him. "We've got to get the canoes down, there's no way to take them out here. Hell, it's easy, just a nice easy boat ride. I've done it a hundred times." He looked at Charles with a challenging smile. "What about it Charles?"

Charles had plenty of white water experience, but he didn't know the Big Blue and he did not relish the ride in pitch blackness. He also worried about his young wife. He knew that as bowman, she would see the chutes first. But Charles had spoken to Jack earlier about his canoeing experience and he felt he could not back down. He agreed.

With Charles on his side, Jack tried cajoling Phil. "C'mon, you'll like it really. Nothing like it...something you'll remember for a long time."

Phil, earlier, when it was not quite dark, had walked down to the chute at the end of the landing. The white plume was at least two feet high and he had heard from Jack that there were others just as menacing downstream.

The vision of the chute came to him now and struck new fear into him. He felt cowardly. He blushed and started to feel warm. He didn't know how to get out of this.

His wife, intoxicated by the fresh air and sufficient amount of alcohol, approached him. "Don't be chicken, Phil. It'll be fun."

Her siding with the others was the last straw. Phil screamed, "You take the bloody canoe, then. I wouldn't go through those chutes for anything, anytime. Now it's suicide."

Wendell heard all of the conversation. He stood up puffing and smiling. "Hell, I'll take the goddam thing down for him." He handed Phil the key to his car. "Here, you take my car back with Sadie. Jack will need a bowman in the lead canoe, so I think that Carol should go with Jack."

Carol was excited, and the idea of bowman in the lead canoe thrilled her. "C'mon what are we waiting for. Let's go."

V.

They were gone hooting and shouting as they flew over the first chute. Phil and Sadie packed up the remaining groceries, utensils and liquor bottles, cleaned Perkins gazebo and started up the steep hill to the pickup. Wendell's Grand Prix was parked at the log road entrance to the hard road. Sadie said she would drive Phil to Wendell's car and they got in the pickup. She started the old machine and ground the gears noisily, trying to drive the pickup away in second. It did not respond, and by the time she found first, the machine was hopelessly mired in the sand.

"C'mon, leave it here. We'll go back in Wendell's car."

By road, the ride back to the shop took less than 20 minutes.

When they got there, they had another drink and sat down. Phil relaxed in his chair. He was glad to be alone with Sadie, and he asked her personal questions about herself and Jack. She responded willingly. They met at the northern branch of the state university. He was in art, then went away to study in Chicago. She was a music student and had studied piano for years. When Jack returned, they decided to get married against the wishes of his parents. They didn't like her style of living, although it was exactly the same as Jack's. They didn't think a guide and tackle shop on the remote Big Blue was a good business idea for a person with Jack's talents. They also thought the purchase of the rundown house was ridiculous, even though they put up the down payment for it. Nobody lived the way they did, nowadays.

Sadie continued. It was the parents who made a fisherman out of Jack. They brought him up here on the Big Blue when he was only five years old. They owned a large, summer cottage on the river, and he was there every summer since. What could they expect him to do, now?

Through the opened, screened window, Phil thought he heard something.

"I think we should walk down to the river. They might be coming."

"They should be getting close, now."

They left the room and walked down to the edge of the river. It was quiet and a moon came out lighting the gravelly take-out like a search light. The river revealed, Phil worried about his wife.

"I hope nothing happened."

Sadie was not worried. This was their life style. They had done this before many times and in the same inebriated condition. "They'll be here. Jack will bring them home safely."

Now, up river in the darkness, they could hear them.

"Hoot, hoot, hoot." Laughter. "Hoot, hoot, hoot."

"Jack's calling owls. He's good at it. They really answer him."

A great sense of relief came over Phil, and he was looking forward to seeing the group and his wife again. They wouldn't be in such a jovial mood if anything serious had happened.

Jack's canoe appeared first, Carol sitting upright in bowman's position, paddle crossed on her lap. She was smiling as Jack ground the canoe up the bank. Phil helped her out.

"How was it?"

"Oh, you missed it. It was beautiful and exciting. Jack really knows the river. Right down the middle of every chute, just like a roller coaster. Jack calls owls...did you hear him?"

Jack came up drunker now than before he left. He cupped his mouth with his hands. "Hoot." "Hoot." "I really had them talking to me tonight. Showed Carol every spring in the Big Blue. Undignified to drink bourbon without branchwater. Wendell got plenty of it though. He went in."

The second canoe pulled up. It was Charles and his wife. She was ashen. Phil went over to help them out.

"How was it Chuck?"

"Real hairy. You were right not to come down. My wife cried when Wendell went in. He needed a bowman, didn't have a chance without one. He's ok. We pulled over in the eddy and helped him right the canoe. He drank all the way down after that. Pretty drunk, now. Here he comes."

Wendell ground the canoe hard on the gravel, stroking the shallow bottom with the paddle. He got out. His clothes, now partially dried, were tight on his thighs and biceps. Phil went over to help. "Thanks a lot for bringing the canoe down. I'm sorry to hear you went in."

Wendell glowered at him. "Next time stay off the goddam river."

Jack came up intervening. "Hey, we're all ok, now. It's a beautiful night. Let's go up to the house and dry out Wendell."

As they approached the house, Jack noticed that the truck was not parked in its usual position. "What happened to the truck?"

Sadie replied, "Oh, I got it stuck. We came home in the Grand Prix."

Jack was irate. "We've got to go back up there and get it out tonight. We need the truck in the morning. And what about all the gear?"

Wendell offered to help. "I'll run you up in my car."

Phil heard them talking. "It's in pretty good, Jack. Why don't we wait until morning. Chuck and I will go up with you and help get it out."

"No, I've got to get it out tonight. You can stay behind, if you like."

"Oh, we'll go with you now, you're going to need all the help you can get."

Jack ran drunkenly into a nearby shed and came back with a couple of shovels and a tow rope. He threw the equipment into the trunk and they all got in the Grand Prix. Wendell backed up the big car and misjudged a tree behind it, putting a pretty good dent in the bumper. They all got out to look at it.

"Son of a bitch. My new car!"

They got back in and started out, Wendell driving fast and furiously, spitting sand and gravel behind them.

They arrived at the log road turn off in a short time and decided to leave the car on the hard, safe road.

The pickup was stuck in the sand 300 yards from the main

dirt road and the four of them walked down the log road to the pickup.

Chuck and Phil engineered the problem quickly. Jack and Wendell were too drunk to be of much help with the engineering, but could do as they were told by Chuck and Phil. Together, they jacked up the pickup, shoveled loose sand out, spread felled branches under it and carried in some big rocks. The pickup was lowered.

"You can get in now, Jack. We'll push." Phil said.

Jack started the engine. He waited briefly and put the pickup in gear. He gunned the motor and with the new traction, started driving the pickup down the log road. He was doing well, but going too fast, when he scraped a large tree and stopped again, mired in deep sand. The others came up. Chuck and Phil knew they would never get the truck out now without a tow truck.

Wendell said, "I'll bring the Grand Prix down here and get the son of a bitch out."

"If you come down here with your car, you'll get stuck, too, and we won't get out of here until morning." Phil said.

"What the hell do you know?" Wendell said threateningly.

In his drunken state, Wendell marched first in one direction and then another towards his automobile. In a few moments, he arrived in it, backing the big car within a few feet of the truck. Chuck and Phil cooperated with Wendell. They tied the tow rope to the Pontiac and then to the truck. Phil hopped into the truck, and pushed Jack over to the passenger side. "I'll drive. Why don't you get out and help push." He stumbled out and went to the rear of the truck with Chuck.

Wendell sat in his car, revving the powerful motor. He signaled to Phil and they tried to get out with full power in both vehicles. The Pontiac strained against the tow rope and churned itself deeper and deeper into the sand, and it was obvious that the Pontiac was mired hopelessly, too.

Out of the car, Wendell marched furiously toward the pickup. When he reached Phil getting out, he screamed. "You bastard, you don't know how to drive, either."

"Relax, we'll get you out, but the truck will have to stay."

Chuck and Phil repeated the process of jacking the car up, digging out, spreading rocks and lowering the Pontiac. They were ready and motioned to Wendell to drive it out.

He had little feeling in his foot on the gas pedal and he revved the engine unmercifully. The car quickly sank back in its original place.

They repeated the process a couple of times and it was obvious to Phil and Chuck they would never get the big car out of the sand with Wendell at the wheel. Chuck said, "We've got to get him out of the car or we'll never get out."

"I'll ask him." Phil said.

Phil went over to Wendell. "Why don't you let me try it?"

"No son of a bitch is taking this car out of here but me."

"Ok, but take it a little slower next time."

Phil and Chuck went at it again. During each preceding try the Grand Prix had moved slightly ahead onto harder ground. They motioned to Wendell to try once more.

He pressed the gas pedal more slowly and started to climb right up and out of the sand. When he realized he was out, he gunned the engine and roared down the narrow, twisting log road in a blaze of sand and gravel. He scraped a tree, damaging the side of the Pontiac and stopped down the road on the hard ground. He got out, looked at the new damage to his car and marched back to Phil and Chuck with fists clenched.

Phil and Chuck each picked up a shovel and walked

towards Wendell. Phil put his arm around Jack. "C'mon, we're going home."

They were met halfway to the car by Wendell, enraged. He charged at Phil, ominously, big fists raised. "I want you, you little bastard. C'mon."

Phil was livid. He didn't want to fight the enraged and drunken Wendell. He feared him, but he could not control his fear. It left him and he swung hard with the shovel into Wendell's ribs. His fists came down as he sank to his knees in the soft sand. The blow knocked the wind out of him, and he lay doubled up holding his ribs and moaning from the pain.

Chuck and Jack lifted Wendell, but he could not straighten up and they half carried him and dragged him to the car.

Jack, sobered slightly by the event, came back for Phil.

"I'm very sorry about all this. He had it coming. Let's go back to the house."

"I won't ride with him. I'll walk back."

"It's 12 miles."

"I don't give a damn. I just want to walk. Leave me alone."

Jack left him on the sandy log road and went back to the car. Phil watched it pull away, the red taillights twisting back and forth slowly through the trees.

He started to walk towards the hard road and looked up into the sky. In the east, it was getting quite light.